1

Gra
in practice

with key

Jennifer Seidl

Oxford University Press

Oxford University Press
Walton Street, Oxford OX2 6DP

Oxford New York Toronto
Petaling Jaya Singapore Hong Kong Tokyo
Delhi Bombay Madras Calcutta Karachi
Nairobi Dar es Salaam Cape Town
Melbourne Auckland

and associated companies in
Beirut Berlin Ibadan Nicosia

OXFORD is a trade mark
of Oxford University Press

ISBN 0 19 432719 1

First published 1981
Eighth impression 1987

Phototypeset in Linotron Sabon by
Filmtype Services Limited, Scarborough

Printed in Hong Kong

Contents

Introduction

This grammar exercise-book has been written for adolescents and adults who are beginning to learn English. It therefore includes essential structures and grammar items at an elementary to pre-intermediate level.

The book is subdivided into sections, each dealing with more than one grammar point. When the grammar point can give rise to special difficulties, it is presented in stages and recurs in other sections of the book. Full cross-referencing allows the student to find the separate parts of the same grammar item with ease.

Each section begins with a short dialogue, narrative, or letter, which illustrates the grammar point and presents it in context. The grammar item is then summarized by means of a short and simple explanation, table, list, or diagram. As far as possible, grammar labels have been avoided in the explanations and only appear as headings for reference purposes. After the grammar summary, there are several varied exercises on each point. In the early sections, exercises are controlled without being mechanical, but they become more demanding as the student progresses. A unique feature of this approach is that most of the exercises, with a few exceptions, have been contextualized. Thus, the student is not presented with the traditional long lists of isolated sentences. All exercises are headed by examples.

There is no story-line, but most of the exercises relate to the same group of characters, who provide situations for the grammar items in neutral or informal language.

There is a key at the end of the book for students working on their own.

1 Be: present
Possessive adjectives

Who's that?

Hello! My name's Steve Baxter. And I'm Jill Baxter.

A Excuse me, please. Is your name Baxter?
B Yes, it is. I'm Steve Baxter. And this is my wife, Jill.
A Oh, good. How do you do?

C Hello! You're Jill Baxter.
D Yes, that's right. I am. And this is my husband, Steve.
C Oh, good. How are you?
D Fine, thanks.

E Excuse me, please, but is your name Bill Blake?
F No, I'm sorry, it isn't. It's Baxter, Steve Baxter.
E Oh, I'm so sorry.

G Excuse me, please, but are you Janet Blake?
H No, I'm sorry, I'm not. My name's Jill Baxter.
G Oh, sorry.

Jill and Steve

Steve Baxter is a journalist in London.
He's a busy man. His work is very interesting.

Jill Baxter is a teacher at a language school in London.
She's a busy woman. Her work is very interesting, too.

Be: present (singular)

I am	Am I . . .?	I am not
You are	Are you . . .?	You are not
He is	Is he . . .?	He is not
She is	Is she . . .?	She is not
It is	Is it . . .?	It is not

Note 1
All persons are *he* or *she*, all things are *it*.
He is a busy man.
She is a busy woman.
It is a language school.

Note 2
I: always with a capital letter.

Short forms (in speech and informal writing)

I'm	I'm not
You're	You aren't (you're not)
He's	He isn't (he's not)
She's	She isn't (she's not)
It's	It isn't (it's not)

Short answers

Are you Steve Baxter?	Yes, I am.	No, I'm not.
Is he Steve Baxter?	Yes, he is.	No, he isn't.
Is your name Blake?	Yes, it is.	No, it isn't.

Note: 'Yes, I'm', etc. is wrong. Say 'Yes, I am'.

Possessive adjectives: singular

I'm Jill Baxter, and this is *my* husband, Steve.
You're Steve Baxter, and is that *your* wife?
He's a journalist and *his* work is very interesting.
She's a teacher and *her* work is very interesting, too.

Note 1
A before a singular countable noun.
a man a woman a language school

Note 2
Adjectives: only one form.
a good journalist   a good wife   a good language school

Note 3
Position of *too*: at the end.
Jill is a teacher. Mary is a teacher.
Jill is a teacher and Mary is a teacher, too.

Exercise 1

Am, are, is.

1 A ____ Jill a teacher?
B Yes, she ____.
A ____ you a teacher, too, Steve?
B Oh, no! I ____ a journalist.
A ____ that interesting work?
B Oh, yes! It ____!
2 C ____ you Jill Baxter?
D Yes, that ____ right. I ____.

Exercise 2

Use short forms.

A Excuse me, please, but is your name Bill Blake?
B No, it is not. I am sorry.
A You are not Bill Blake?
B No, I am not.
A Are you Steve Baxter, the journalist?
B Yes, that is right, I am!

Exercise 3

I, my, you, your, he, his, she, her, it.

A Hello, is ____ name Blake?
B No, ____ isn't. ____ am sorry. ____ name's Baxter, Steve Baxter.
A Oh! (to Jill) But ____ are Mrs Janet Blake!
C No, sorry. ____ am Jill Baxter, ____ wife. ____ is ____ husband.
A Oh, so sorry . . . ! Hmm! ____ isn't Bill Blake! ____ name's Baxter!
And ____ isn't Janet Blake! ____ name's Jill Baxter!

Exercise 4

Use short answers.

Is he Bill Blake? *No, he isn't.*
Are you Steve Baxter? *Yes, I am.*

1 Is Steve Baxter a teacher?
2 Is he a journalist?
3 Is his work interesting?
4 Is Janet Blake his wife?
5 Is Jill Baxter his wife?
6 Is Steve a busy man?
7 Is Jill Baxter a journalist?
8 Is Jill a busy woman?
9 Is her work interesting, too?
10 Is the language school in London?
11 Are you a busy man/woman?
12 Is your work interesting?

2 Be: present Possessive adjectives Question words

In class

Jill Good morning. My name's Jill Baxter. I'm your English teacher. Welcome to London and to our school. Now, what are your names, please?
Ali My name's Mr Badran.
Jill And what's your first name, please? I'm Jill, not Mrs Baxter. First names in class!
Ali OK. I'm Ali. I'm from Egypt.
Jill Thank you, Ali. And who are you, please?
Monika I'm Monika Wengli from Brugg.
Jill Where's that? Is it in Germany?
Monika No, it isn't. It's in Switzerland, near Zürich.
Jill Thank you, Monika. And where are you from, please?
Annegret I'm from Germany. My name's Annegret Wade.
Jill Wade? But that's English.
Annegret Yes, that's right. I'm married to an Englishman.

What are their names?

Surname	First name	Country
Mr Badran	Ali	Egypt
Mr Berger	Maurice	France
Mr Deng	Chu Wen	China
Miss Dubois	Pascale	Switzerland
Miss de Lacerda	Luisa	Brazil
Mr Manolatos	Mikis	Greece
Mr Mazouni	Halim	Algeria
Miss Mendoza	María	Mexico
Mrs Olsen	Astrid	Sweden
Mr Pérez	Juan	Spain
Miss Tanaka	Yasuko	Japan
Mr Torrini	Enrico	Italy
Mrs Wade	Annegret	Germany
Miss Wengli	Monika	Switzerland

Monday morning

Jill Good morning! Are we all here? No, who's missing?
María Enrico and Luisa are missing.
Jill Yes, that's right. They're late. I hope they aren't ill. Ah, here they are now. Good. Hello!
Enrico Good morning. Sorry we're late.
Jill Oh, that's all right. I'm glad you're here. Are you both OK?
Enrico No, we aren't. Luisa has a cold and I have a headache. It's your English weather!

Be: present (plural)

We	are	Are	we . . .?	We	are not
You			you . . .?	You	
They			they . . .?	They	

Short forms (in speech and informal writing)

We're	We aren't (we're not)
You're	You aren't (you're not)
They're	They aren't (they're not)

Short answers

Are you OK?	Yes, we are.	No, we aren't.
Are we late?	Yes, you are.	No, you aren't.
Are they missing?	Yes, they are.	No, they aren't.

Note: 'Yes, we're', etc. is wrong. Say 'Yes, we are'.

Possessive adjectives: plural

Welcome to *our* school.	we	our
What are *your* names?	you	your
Their names are Ali and Halim.	they	their

Note
Plural of nouns: *noun + s*.
name names

Question words with is

What's . . .?	Who's . . .?	Where's . . .?	How's . . .?
What's your name?	Who's missing?	Where's Brugg?	How's Luisa?

No short forms with *am* and *are*:
What are your names? Who are you? Where am I? How are you?

Note
Both
Luisa is late. Enrico is late. They are both late.

Exercise 5

Am, are, is.

Jill Hello. _____ we all here today? No, who _____ missing?
María Enrico _____ missing and Luisa _____ missing, too.
Jill Yes, they _____late. I hope they _____ not ill.
Enrico Good morning! Here I _____.
Luisa Sorry I _____ late.
Jill Oh, that _____ all right. _____ you both OK?

Exercise 6

We, our, you, your, they, their.

1 **Jill** Pascale and Monika, what are _____ surnames, please?
Monika _____ surnames are Dubois and Wengli. _____ are from Switzerland. I'm from Brugg, near Zürich, and Pascale is from Geneva.
Jill Are _____ married?
Monika No, _____ aren't.
2 **Steve** The students from Switzerland, what are _____ names, Jill?
Jill Pascale and Monika.
Steve Are _____both from Geneva?
Jill No, _____ aren't.

Exercise 7

Complete.

Name	Country	Married
Juan	Spain	Yes
Annegret		
Pascale		
María		
Astrid		
Monika		

Use short answers.

Are Pascale and Monika both married? *No, they aren't.*

1 Are Juan and María both from Spain?
2 Pascale and Monika, are you both from Switzerland?
3 Monika and María, are you both married?
4 Are Astrid and Annegret both married?
5 Are Annegret and Monika both from Germany?
6 Juan and Astrid, are you both married?
7 Are Enrico and Luisa both late?
8 Enrico and Luisa, are you both OK?

Exercise 8

What's, how's, where's, who's, where are, how are.

1 **A** Brugg? _____ that?
B Near Zürich.
2 **C** _____ missing?
D Enrico and Luisa.
3 **E** _____ Enrico and Luisa?
F They're missing.
4 **G** _____ you?
H Fine, thanks.
G And _____ your wife?
H Oh, she's fine, too, thank you.
5 **I** _____ your name, please?
J Monika.

Exercise 9

Use short answers.

1 Is Astrid Olsen married?
2 Is Brugg in Germany?
3 Are Yasuko Tanaka and Deng Chu Wen both from Japan?
4 Is Juan from Mexico?
5 Is María Mendoza married?
6 Are Pascale and Monika both from Switzerland?
7 Is Enrico from Italy?
8 Is Luisa from Brazil?
9 Is Brugg in Switzerland?
10 Maurice, is your name Dubois?
11 Juan and María, are you both from Spain?
12 Yasuko, are you from China?

Exercise 10

Use short forms.

Jill _____ missing? Enrico?
María Yes, Enrico and Luisa are missing.
Jill Yes, _____ late. I hope _____ ill.
Enrico Good morning. _____ both late! Sorry!
Jill _____ OK. I'm glad _____ here now. Are you all right?
Enrico No, _____.

3 There is, there are Some, any

How many students are there?

Steve How many students are there in your class, Jill?
Jill There are fourteen altogether.
Steve Are there any students from Venezuela?
Jill No, there aren't any from Venezuela. Not in my class.
Steve Oh, I'm surprised. There are usually some students from Venezuela.
Jill There are some from Asia. There's a student from Japan, and there's a student from China, too.
Steve And is there a student from Thailand this time?
Jill No, there isn't. But there's one from Mexico.
Steve But I expect there are some Dutch students.
Jill No, there aren't. But there's one from Brazil.
Steve Is there a student from Sweden?
Jill Yes, there is. She's a very pretty girl! But she's married, Steve, and you are, too!

There is, there are

Singular:	There is	Is there . . .?	There is not
Plural:	There are	Are there . . .?	There are not

Short forms

Singular:	There's	There isn't
Plural:	No short form	There aren't

Short answers

Is there a student from Thailand?
Yes, there is.
No, there isn't.

Are there any students from Africa?
Yes, there are.
No, there aren't.

Note: 'Yes, there's' is wrong. Say 'Yes, there is'.

Some, any

Singular

There's *a* student from Africa.

Is there *a* student from Africa?
Yes, there is. (or Yes, there's *one* from Egypt.)
No, there isn't.

Plural

There are *some* students from South America.

Are there *any* students from Brazil?
Yes, there are *some*.
No, there are*n't any*.

Note

Remember: *some* in affirmative sentences.
any in questions and negatives.

Exercise 11

There is, there are.

Is there a student from Sweden in the class? *Yes, there is.*
Are there any students from Argentina? *No, there aren't.*

1 Is there a student from Mexico in the class?
2 Is there a student from Thailand?
3 Are there any students from Switzerland?
4 Are there any students from Holland?
5 Is there a student from Venezuela?
6 Is there a student from Brazil?
7 Are there any students from Norway?
8 Are there any students from Asia?
9 Is there a student from Italy?
10 Are there any students from India?
11 Is there a student from China?
12 Are there any married students?
13 Is there a student from Belgium?
14 Is there a student from Greece?
15 Are there any students from Portugal?

Exercise 12

There is, there are, there isn't, there aren't, is there, are there?

Harry *Are there* any students from India in your class?
Jill No, *there aren't.* _____ two students from Latin America, but _____ any from Venezuela and _____ a student from Argentina this year. _____ a young lady from Japan, _____ two from Switzerland and _____ a student from Greece.
Harry _____ a student from Italy?
Jill Yes, _____.
Harry _____ any students from Norway?
Jill No, _____. Not this year.

Exercise 13

Some, any, one.

Steve Are there _____ students from Switzerland in your class, Jill?
Jill Yes, there are two, but there aren't _____ from Holland. There are _____ students from Asia this time. There's _____ from Japan, a young lady, and there's _____ from China, a man. There are usually _____ students from Venezuela, but there aren't _____ this time.
Steve Are there _____ from South America?
Jill Yes, there's _____ from Brazil, a young lady.
Steve And are there _____ from France?
Jill Yes, there's _____ from France, a man.
Steve Are there _____ students from Scandinavia?
Jill Yes, there's _____ from Sweden, Astrid. And there are _____ married students. Astrid is married.

4 Have got
Imperative

A phone call

Jill (on the phone) Hello, Steve. It's Jill. I've got a free afternoon. Have you got enough time for lunch with me?
Steve No, I'm sorry, Jill, I haven't. Why?
Jill Well, I've got a newspaper advertisement here. It's for a flat in Hampstead. It's got two bedrooms, a modern kitchen, central heating . . .
Steve And has it got a garage?
Jill Yes, it has.
Steve I'm sure it has, Jill, but we haven't got enough money!

A day in bed

Steve I've got a headache and a temperature.
Jill Oh, dear. Stay at home then. Perhaps you've got flu. Go back to bed and take some tablets.
Steve Yes, that's a good idea.
Jill Or phone Dr Ray.

Have got

I You We They	have	got	Have	I you we they	got . . .?	I You We They	have not	got
He She It	has	got	Has	he she it	got . . .?	He She It	has not	got

Short forms

I've	got	I	haven't	got
You've		You		
We've		We		
They've		They		
He's	got	He	hasn't	got
She's		She		
It's		It		

Short answers

Have you got a flat?	Yes, I have.	No, I haven't.
Has it got a garage?	Yes, it has.	No, it hasn't.
Have we got enough money?	Yes, we have.	No, we haven't.

Use

In the present tense we often use *have* or *has* with *got*. It means 'possess'.
I've got a car.

Imperative: affirmative

There is only one form for singular and plural.
Stay at home then.
Take some tablets.

Note
Enough + noun
I haven't got enough money.
There aren't enough eggs.

Exercise 14

Have, haven't, has, hasn't.

Sports Centre
swimming-pool
tennis-courts
squash-courts
yoga room
lecture room
cafeteria

Adult classes	
Keep fit	Monday 7pm
Yoga	Wednesday 6pm
Photography	Wednesday 7pm
Guitar	Tuesday 7pm
Cookery	Friday 8pm
French	Thursday 7pm

Jill Look, Steve, a new sports centre.
Steve Great. It _____ got a swimming-pool.
Jill Yes, and tennis-courts.
Steve And it _____ got a yoga room.
Jill Good! They _____ got a yoga class on Wednesdays.
Steve They _____ got a French class, but they _____ got a Spanish class. Pity!
Jill Oh, and look Steve, they _____ got a photography class, too. Very interesting.
Steve But they _____ got a gardening class . . .
Jill And we _____ got a garden.
Steve It _____ got table tennis, it _____ got volleyball . . .
Jill And you _____ got enough time.

Exercise 15

Flat in Hampstead. Two bedrooms, modern kitchen, new bathroom, garage, central heating, telephone.

Use short answers: *Yes, he has, No, he hasn't*, etc.

1 Has Jill got a free afternoon?
2 Has Steve got time for lunch with Jill?
3 Has the flat got central heating?
4 Has it got five bedrooms?
5 Has it got a garage?
6 Has it got a big balcony?
7 Have Jill and Steve got enough money for the flat?
8 Has Steve got a car?
9 Have you got a flat with five bedrooms?
10 Have you got a car?

Exercise 16

Match the car and the owner.

The student from Germany has got a Renault. The student from France has got a French car, too. The student from Mexico hasn't got a French car. The students from Sweden and France have got the same car. The student from France hasn't got a Renault.

María	Volkswagen
Maurice	Renault
Annegret	Citroën
Astrid	

Now ask questions with *have got, has got.*

1 Maurice, a Renault?
2 María, a German car?
3 Astrid, a Fiat?
4 Maurice and Astrid, a French car?
5 Annegret, a Citroën?
6 María and Annegret, a Volkswagen?

Exercise 17

Come, open, phone, say, stay, take.

Dr Ray _____ your mouth, please, Mr Baxter. Fine. And now _____ 'Ah'. Yes, good. You've got flu. _____ in bed until Wednesday and ____ this medicine. _____ me tomorrow morning, please and ____ and see me on Thursday. It isn't serious. Goodbye.

Steve Thank you, doctor. Goodbye.

Exercise 18

Add, bake, beat, cool, cream, mash, put, serve.

Banana loaf

115 g sugar
1 egg
85 g butter
2 bananas
225 g flour

_____ the sugar and the butter. _____ in the egg. _____ the bananas. _____ the flour. _____ into a tin and _____ for 30 minutes. _____ and _____.

5 Object pronouns Simple present Word order

Steve at work

Steve I work for the Daily News. The work is interesting and I enjoy it. I travel a lot. My office is in Fleet Street. I share it with Barbara Robson. She's new and I help her. My boss is Mr Short. I like him. Mr Short and my friend, Harry Turner, help me with difficult articles, and I help them, too. We are all very busy people.

Free time

Steve We don't go out during the week, but we do at the weekend. We visit friends, or they visit us. On Saturday evenings, we go to our favourite pub. On Sundays, we visit our relations in the country.
Jill Unfortunately, we haven't got time for sport.
Steve Oh, yes, we have! We run for the bus every morning!

Questions at lunch-time

Barbara Do you and Jill eat at a restaurant at the weekend?
Steve Yes, we do. We know a very good Indian restaurant. We like Chinese food, too.
Barbara Do you cook it at home?
Steve Yes, I do, but it isn't easy!
Barbara Do your friends like Chinese food?
Steve No, they don't like it very much, not *my* Chinese food . . .

Object pronouns

You help *me*.	Our friends visit *us*.
I help *you*.	Your friends visit *you*.
He's nice. I like *him*.	We visit *them*.
She's nice. I help *her*.	
My work is interesting. I enjoy *it*.	

Note: For persons *him*, *her*, and *them*. For things *it* and *them*.

Simple present: I, you, we, they

I You We They	help her.	Do	I you we they	help her?	I You We They	do not (don't)	help her.

Short answers

Do you help her? Yes, I do. No, I don't.
Yes, we do. No, we don't, etc.

Use

general facts
I enjoy my work.
We like Chinese food very much.

repeated actions and habits
We run for the bus every morning.
They don't smoke.

truths
Dogs bark.

Word order

subject	verb	object
I	like	him.
We	visit	them.

The usual order is *subject + verb + object*. There is nothing between the verb and the object.

Exercise 19

Me, you, him, her, it, us, them.

Steve Mr Short is a nice man. I like ____. Mr Short and Harry Turner help ____ with difficult articles.
Jill And Barbara Robson? Do you like ____?
Steve Yes, she's nice. She's new, so I help ____. I have a nice office now and I share ____ with Barbara.
Jill My students are very nice, too. I like ____.
Steve And do they like ____?
Jill Oh, yes. They like ____ and Julia. They like ____ very much. And our classroom is nice, too. We love ____.

Exercise 20

Cook, go, help, know, like, run, share, visit, work.

1 I _____ for the Daily News.
2 My office is in Fleet Street. I _____ it with Barbara Robson.
3 Barbara is new, so I _____ her.
4 Jill and Steve _____ out at the weekend.
5 On Sundays, they _____ their relations in the country.
6 They _____Chinese food. They _____ it at home.
7 We _____ a very good Indian restaurant.
8 We like sport! We _____ for the bus every morning!

Exercise 21

Ask questions.

I enjoy my work. (you?)
Do you enjoy your work?
Jill and Steve know a good Indian restaurant. (Barbara and Harry?)
Do Barbara and Harry know a good Indian restaurant?

1 I go to bed early. (you?)
2 We like Chinese food. (Jill and Steve?)
3 I share my office. (you?)
4 We like English tea. (the students?)
5 Jill and Steve watch television every evening. (we?)
6 Jill and Steve visit their relations in the country. (I?)
7 They don't find much time for sport. (you?)
8 Jill and Steve love Indian food. (their friends?)
9 They run for the bus every morning. (we?)
10 I go out during the week. (Jill and Steve?)

Exercise 22

Complete.

Steve Is *that* a new dress?
Jill Yes. _____ you (like) it?
Steve Yes, _____.
Jill Thanks.
Steve And _____ you (like) my new tie?
Jill No, _____. It's horrible.
Steve But you like blue ties.
Jill But I _____ (like) *that* tie.
Steve Don't you?
Jill No, _____.
Steve _____ you (like) my new shirt?

Jill Yes, _____. It's very nice.
Steve I'm glad. Jill, _____ you (want) a cup of tea?
Jill No, _____, thanks.

Exercise 23

Make sentences, as in the example.

very much, our friends, Chinese food, don't like
Our friends don't like Chinese food very much.

1 at the weekend, eat, at a restaurant, we
2 enjoy, very much, we, Chinese food
3 at home, we, it, cook
4 our relations, we, on Sundays, visit, in the country
5 we, our favourite pub, on Saturday evenings, go to

6 The indefinite article Simple present This, that

Occupations

Name	Occupation
Dr Ali Badran	doctor of medicine
Mr Maurice Berger	student
Dr Deng Chu Wen	doctor of chemistry
Miss Pascale Dubois	art teacher
Miss Luisa de Lacerda	air hostess
Mr Mikis Manolatos	architect
Mr Halim Mazouni	engineer
Miss María Mendoza	secretary
Mrs Astrid Olsen	student
Mr Juan Pérez	businessman
Miss Yasuko Tanaka	student
Mr Enrico Torrini	journalist
Mrs Annegret Wade	interpreter, now housewife
Miss Monika Wengli	travel guide

A photograph

Jill Look, Steve, I've got a picture here of my students. That's Halim, an engineer. He works for an oil company. And that's Enrico. He's a journalist. He writes for an Italian newspaper in Milan. And that's Luisa, an air hostess. She travels all over the world with an American airline. This is Juan, a businessman from Madrid. He exports Spanish antiques, an unusual job. And here's Mikis. He designs houses in Athens. And that's Monika from Switzerland. She's a travel guide for an international tourist organization. She speaks four languages.

Steve It all sounds very interesting, Jill. But where's Astrid, the very pretty girl?

Jill Sorry, Steve, but she isn't in this picture.

Questions

Steve Does María work for an airline?
Jill No, she doesn't, Steve. That's Luisa. María works for Volkswagen.
Steve Oh, yes, that's right. And does Mikis design houses in Athens?
Jill Yes, he does.
Steve And Enrico exports antiques.
Jill No, he doesn't! That's Juan!
Steve Wrong again! I'm not a good student, Jill.

The indefinite article: a, an

an	before *a*, *e*, *i*, *o*, *u*	an American airline an English company an Italian newspaper an oil company an unusual job
an	before mute *h*	an hour
a	before a *y sound*	a usual job a university

Use

Singular
The indefinite article comes before an occupation.
He's a journalist.
She's an interpreter.

Plural
There is no article in the plural.
They are journalists.
They are interpreters.

Simple present: he, she, it

He export*s* antiques.
She speak*s* four languages.
It rain*s* a lot here.

Does	he	export . . .?	
	she	speak . . .?	
	it	rain . . .?	

He	does not	export . . .
She	(doesn't)	speak . . .
It		rain . . .

Short answers

Does he export antiques? Yes, he does. No, he doesn't, etc.

Remember: *he*, *she*, *it* + *verb* + *s* in the affirmative.

This, that

Singular

This is Luisa. That is (that's) Enrico.
This is a language school. That is (that's) a flat.

Plural

These are my brother and sister. Those are my students.
These are offices. Those are flats.

	Near	Far
Singular	this	that
Plural	these	those

Exercise 24

Complete with *a* or *an*.

1 Luisa has got _____ very interesting job.
2 She's _____ air hostess.
3 She works for _____ big airline, _____ American airline.
4 She likes to work for _____ airline, but not in _____ office.
5 Is there _____ Italian student in your class, Jill?
6 What does Annegret do? She's _____ interpreter, but at the moment she's _____ housewife.
7 Yasuko is _____ student of English at _____ university in Japan.
8 Juan has _____ unusual job.
9 Annegret is married to _____ Englishman.
10 Have you got time for lunch? Yes, I have. About _____ hour.

Exercise 25

Answer as in the examples.

What do you do, Ali? *I'm a doctor.*
What does Luisa do? *She's an air hostess.*

1 What does Mikis do?
2 What does Pascale do?
3 What does Enrico do?
4 What do you do, Halim?
5 What do Maurice, Yasuko, and Astrid do?
6 What do you do, Monika?
7 What does Juan do?
8 What do you do, María?

Exercise 26

Complete with: *designs*, *exports*, *speaks*, *works*, *writes*.

Steve Deng Chu Wen _____ in Peking. Is that right, Jill? And Mikis _____ houses in Athens. And Enrico _____ antiques, María _____ four languages and Maurice _____ for an Italian newspaper. Is that right, Jill?

Jill Oh, Steve! And Juan is an air hostess . . .!

Exercise 27

Complete.

Luisa sits between Maurice and Chu Wen. On the right of Yasuko is Mikis. Juan sits on the left of Pascale. There is a student from France on the right of Monika. Pascale sits behind Maurice. Yasuko sits between Mikis and Pascale.

1 _____	2 _____	3 _____	4 _____
5 _____	6 Pascale	7 _____	8 _____

Now answer these questions. Use short answers: *Yes, he does. No, he doesn't*, etc.

1 Does Yasuko sit between Juan and Pascale?
2 Does Mikis sit behind Chu Wen?
3 Does Juan sit on the right of Maurice?
4 Does Luisa sit on the left of Chu Wen?
5 Does Pascale sit between Yasuko and Mikis?
6 Does Juan sit behind Monika?
7 Does Pascale teach art?
8 Does Chu Wen work for an oil company?
9 Does Mikis work in Athens?
10 Does Monika export Spanish antiques?
11 Does Juan work for an airline?
12 Does Yasuko study English?
13 Does Halim work for an oil company?
14 Does Maurice work for a newspaper?
15 Does Luisa work for an airline?
16 Does it rain here often?

Exercise 28

Ask questions, as in the examples.

I speak English. (French?)
Do you speak French, too?

Steve listens to the radio every day. (watch television?)
Does he watch television every day, too?

1 They like English tea. (English coffee?)
2 Steve reads The Times. (The Guardian?)
3 They speak English. (other languages?)
4 I like English people. (the English weather?)
5 Steve cooks Chinese food. (Indian food?)
6 Jill and Steve go to bed early. (get up early?)
7 We visit friends at the weekend. (during the week?)
8 Jill and Steve run for the bus every morning. (every evening?)
9 Steve drinks beer. (whisky?)
10 I like English pubs. (English beer?)

Exercise 29

Complete with a preposition.

1 Here's a photograph ____ my students, but Astrid isn't ____ it.
2 Luisa travels all ____ the world.
3 Halim works ____ an oil company.
4 Deng Chu Wen is a doctor ____ chemistry.
5 Mikis designs houses ____ Athens.

Exercise 30

Answer as in the examples.

Is this your coat? *Yes, that's my coat.*
Are these your gloves? *Yes, those are my gloves.*

1 Is this your book?
2 Are these your postcards?
3 Is this your briefcase?
4 Are these your keys?
5 Are these your cigarettes?
6 Is this your newspaper?
7 Are these your pencils?
8 Is this your bag?
9 Are these your magazines?
10 Is this your umbrella?

Exercise 31

Make sentences, as in the examples.

newspaper
This is my newspaper and that's your newspaper.

pencils
These are my pencils and those are your pencils.

1 book
2 postcards
3 dictionary
4 stamps
5 rubber
6 envelopes
7 notebook
8 pen
9 ruler
10 cigarettes

7 Adverbs of frequency The definite article

Before work

Jill usually gets up at a quarter to eight. Steve doesn't often get up before eight o'clock. The alarm-clock wakes them. They usually have coffee and toast for breakfast, but they never have very much time. Jill often runs for the bus, but she seldom arrives late for school. Steve is sometimes late for work. He often takes his toast with him to the office. Before work, they are always in a hurry. They don't usually say much at breakfast, they never have time!

Saturday morning

Steve Here's the post, Jill. There is a postcard and a letter. The letter is for you. The postcard is from Penny and Graham. Penny writes: 'Lovely time here. Museums every day! I don't like history, but the history of Greece is very interesting. The sun shines every day here. The weather is hot, too hot! The people in our hotel are very friendly.'

Adverbs of frequency

always
usually
often
sometimes
seldom
never

before the verb:
Jill *usually* gets up at a quarter to eight.
Jill *seldom* arrives late for school.
Steve doesn't *often* get up before eight o'clock.

after be:
They are *always* in a hurry.
Steve is *sometimes* late for work.
Jill is *seldom* late for school.

The definite article: the

We use *the*

when we refer to a noun a second time:
There are two postcards and *a letter*. (first time)
The letter is for you. (second time)

when we refer to a noun in a particular sense:
Here's *the postman*. (our particular postman)
Steve takes his toast with him to *the office*. (where he works)
I don't like *history* (general) . . .
. . . but *the history* of Greece (particular) is very interesting.
People are very friendly. (general)
The people in our hotel (particular) are very friendly.

where there is only one:
the sun, the North Pole, the weather

Exercise 32

Make sentences, as in the example.

at a quarter to eight, usually, gets up, Jill
Jill usually gets up at a quarter to eight.

1 goes to work, by bus, always, Jill
2 often, gets, Jill, the 8.30 bus
3 she, for school, seldom, late, is
4 don't say, at breakfast, much, Jill and Steve, usually
5 by bus, usually, Steve, too, goes
6 takes, sometimes, he, the Underground
7 always, he, a newspaper, on the bus, reads
8 Jill, on the bus, never reads
9 usually, Steve, The Times, buys
10 doesn't read, he, at the breakfast table, often
11 is, Steve, late for work, sometimes
12 Jill and Steve, in a hurry, always, are

Exercise 33

Make sentences, as in the example.

Here are *two books* and a paper. (important)
The books are important.

1 There are two postcards and *a newspaper*. (old)
2 I've got a letter and *three postcards*. (all from Spain)
3 There are three pencils and *a felt pen*. (black)
4 I've got *a magazine* and a newspaper. (for Harry)
5 There are *two parcels* and a telegram. (from Aunt Susan)

Exercise 34

Attendance: July														
	Day													
Name	1	2	3	4	7	8	9	10	11	14	15	16	17	18
Ali	p	p	p	p	p	a	p	p	p	p	p	a	p	p
Maurice	p	p	p	p	p	l	p	l	p	p	a	p	p	p
Chu Wen	p	p	p	p	p	p	p	p	p	p	p	p	p	p
Pascale	p	l	l	l	p	p	p	l	l	a	p	p	l	l
Luisa	p	p	p	l	p	l	p	p	l	p	p	l	p	p
Mikis	p	a	a	a	p	p	a	a	a	p	p	p	a	p
Halim	p	l	p	p	p	p	p	p	p	l	l	p	l	p
María	p	a	a	p	p	p	p	p	p	p	p	p	p	p
Astrid	p	p	p	p	p	a	p	p	p	a	p	p	p	p
Juan	p	p	p	p	p	l	a	p	p	p	p	p	p	p
Yasuko	p	p	p	p	p	p	p	p	p	p	p	p	p	p
Enrico	p	l	l	l	p	a	l	l	l	l	p	p	l	l
Annegret	p	p	a	p	p	p	a	p	a	p	a	p	a	p
Monika	p	p	p	p	p	p	p	p	p	p	p	p	p	p

a: absent p: present l: late

Write sentences with *always*, *often*, *sometimes*, *seldom*, *never*, as in the examples.

Ali, absent *Ali is seldom absent.*
Chu Wen, present *Chu Wen is always present.*

1 Maurice, late
2 Pascale, late
3 Luisa, late
4 Mikis, absent
5 Halim, absent
6 María, absent
7 Astrid, late
8 Juan, absent
9 Yasuko, present
10 Enrico, late
11 Annegret, absent
12 Monika, absent

Exercise 35

A, the, or –.

Halim _____ weather is terrible here, at home _____ sun shines every day.

María Yes, in Mexico _____ weather is very good, too, and _____ sky is blue.

Halim Is your house here nice?

María Yes, _____ houses in our street are very nice, but it is noisy. _____ boys next door are very noisy.

Halim Well, _____ boys often are.

María I live with _____ family. Tom is _____ doctor, and, as you know, _____ doctors are very busy people. His wife, Mary, is _____ teacher. She is busy too, but they travel a lot. In January they go to _____ South Pole. Where do you live?

Halim Now at _____ hotel.

María But _____ hotels are very expensive.

Halim Yes, that's right.

8 Present continuous Adverbs of time Can

A postcard from Bordeaux

28th July Dear Jill and Steve, We're spending a wonderful holiday in Bordeaux. The sun shines every day, and I'm thinking about you at home. At the moment, Pam's swimming in the pool, the children are playing, and I'm drinking a lovely cool beer at the hotel bar. It's all very expensive here, but it isn't raining. Love, Jeff, Pam, Mark, and Kate.	Mr & Mrs S. Baxter, 34 Cedar Place, London, SW1B 2AN, England.

Can you swim?

Annegret Can you swim?
Astrid Yes, I can, but I can't dive.
Annegret Can you ski?
Astrid No, I can't, but Pascale can.
Annegret Can you play tennis?
Astrid No, but Pascale and Yasuko can. Look, they are playing now. Perhaps they can teach us.

Present continuous

Present tense of be + verb + ing

I am	drinking beer.	It is	raining.
You are		We are	drinking beer.
He is		You are	
She is		They are	

Am I	drinking beer?	Is it	raining?
Are you		Are we	drinking beer?
Is he		Are you	
Is she		Are they	

I am not	drinking beer.	It is not	raining.
You are not		We are not	drinking beer.
He is not		You are not	
She is not		They are not	

Short forms

I'm drinking beer.	I'm not . . .
You're . . .	You aren't . . .
He's . . .	He isn't . . .
She's . . .	She isn't . . .
It's raining.	It isn't . . .
We're drinking beer.	We aren't . . .
You're . . .	You aren't . . .
They're . . .	They aren't . . .

Short answers

Is it raining?	Yes, it is.	No, it isn't.
Are they swimming?	Yes, they are.	No, they aren't, etc.

Use

For actions *now*. Often with *now*, *just now*, *at the moment*, *at present*, *today*, etc.

Note 1
Spelling changes before *ing*

We double	*t*	sit	sitting	after a short vowel
	d	nod	nodding	
	p	stop	stopping	
	b	rub	rubbing	
	n	run	running	
	m	swim	swimming	
	l	travel	travelling	

We omit final	*e*	shine	shining
		have	having

Note 2
Not in the continuous: hate, know, like, love, prefer, remember, seem, understand.

With *see*, *hear*, *smell*, we use *can*.
I can see a bus.
I can hear a noise.

Adverbs of time

at the beginning
Now I'm drinking coffee.
At present they're working.
On Sundays we visit them.

at the end
I'm drinking coffee *now*.
They're working *at present*.
We visit them *on Sundays*.

Can, can't

I	can	swim.	Can	I	swim?	I	cannot	swim.
You				you		You	(can't)	
He				he		He		
She				she		She		
It				it		It		
We				we		We		
You				you		You		
They				they		They		

Short answers

Can he swim?	Yes, he can.	No, he can't.
Can they walk?	Yes, they can.	No, they can't, etc.

Note
There is no *s* with *can*.
There is no *do*/*does* with *can*.

Use

Can expresses ability in the present.

Exercise 36

Answer the questions.

1 What are Jeff and his family doing in Bordeaux?
2 What's Pam doing at the moment?
3 What are the children doing?
4 Who's Jeff thinking about?
5 What's Jeff drinking?
6 What are Pascale and Yasuko doing?

Exercise 37

Use short forms: *Yes, he is*, *No, he isn't*, etc.

1 Is Jeff spending a holiday in Bordeaux?
2 Is Pam playing with the children at the moment?
3 Is Jeff drinking coffee?
4 Are the children swimming?
5 Are they playing?
6 Is it raining?
7 Are Astrid and Annegret playing tennis?
8 Is Pascale playing tennis with Yasuko?

Exercise 38

Ask questions and answer them.

Jill, teach
What's Jill doing at the moment? *She's teaching.*

the students, chat
What are the students doing now? *They're chatting.*

1 Jeff, drink a beer
2 Pam, swim in the sea
3 the children, play
4 Harry, travel
5 Barbara Robson, type an article
6 Mr Short, sit in his office
7 Harry and Steve, waste time
8 Jill, plan lessons
9 the students, write a test
10 you, practise the present continuous

Exercise 39

Can, can't.

Maurice _____ you play a musical instrument?
Juan No, I _____, but my wife _____. She _____ play the piano. Classical music.

Maurice _____ she play jazz, too?
Juan No, but my two brothers _____. They only play jazz. They _____ play classical music.

Exercise 40

Some of the students can speak English and their native language and other foreign languages, too.

Name	Native language	Other languages
Astrid	Swedish	German
Maurice	French	Spanish
Luisa	Portuguese	Spanish
Juan	Spanish	Italian
Deng Chu Wen	Chinese	French
Monika	German	French, Italian
Annegret	German	Russian
Halim	Arabic	French

Ask questions and answer them.

Juan, French? *Can Juan speak French?*
He can't speak French, but he can speak Italian.

1 Annegret, Spanish?
2 Deng Chu Wen, Japanese?
3 Astrid, Danish?
4 Monika, Spanish?
5 Maurice, Italian?
6 Halim, German?
7 Luisa, Italian?
8 Juan, Chinese?

Exercise 41

Complete with a preposition.

It's wonderful here _____ Bordeaux. We're thinking _____ you _____ home _____ London. _____ the moment, Pam's _____ the swimming-pool, and I'm relaxing _____ the hotel bar _____ a glass _____ beer.

Exercise 42

Simple present or present continuous.

You (cook) now?
Are you *cooking* now?
You usually (cook) after 7.
You usually *cook* after 7.

Steve Jill! Where are you? What you (do) at the moment?
Jill I'm in the bathroom. I (wash) my hair.
Steve But today's Thursday. You usually (wash) your hair on Fridays.

(ten minutes later)
Steve Jill! You (wash) your hair now?
Jill No, now I (dry) it. What you (do)?
Steve I (clean) the shoes.
Jill But you usually (clean) them on Saturdays.

(the telephone rings)
Steve Jill! The phone (ring)! Can you come and answer it? Jill!
Jill What you (say), darling? I can't hear you!
Steve The phone (ring)! I can't answer it. I've got shoe polish on my hands!
Jill (stops the hair-dryer) But I can't hear the phone. It (not ring)!
Steve No, not now . . .

Exercise 43

Simple present or present continuous.

Harry Hello, Steve. This is Harry speaking. I (phone) from the office. I know it's late, but I (work) now.
Steve It's almost 10 o'clock! You never (stay) so late! What's wrong?
Harry I (have) difficulty with the article on the rail strike.
Steve But you seldom (have) difficulty with the articles. You always (finish) them quickly.
Harry Steve, what you (do) just now? You (watch) television at the moment?
Steve No, but we're still up. Jill (prepare) lessons for tomorrow, and I (get) ready for bed. But come over, Harry!

9 Spelling Plurals Possession The indefinite article

After work

Jill teaches five hours a day, twenty-five hours a week altogether. She finishes work at about 4 o'clock in the afternoon. Then she catches a bus home. The buses are sometimes very full, so she takes the Underground. Twice a week, on Mondays and Fridays, she goes to a big supermarket. She buys a lot of things there. Steve leaves his office at about 6 o'clock. Then he hurries home. After supper, Steve washes the dishes, and then he reads or spends time on his hobbies. Jill relaxes with a book or a women's magazine, or she sometimes watches a film on television.

The Baxters' flat

Jill and Steve's flat is very nice, but it has a big disadvantage: the neighbours! In the flat below, the neighbours' dog barks every night, and in the flat above, the children's records are very loud. In the flat next door the neighbour's wife practises the trumpet every evening, so Steve and Jill always go to their parents' house in the country at the weekend.

Spelling

With a final *-ch*, *-sh*, *-s*, *-z*, *-x*

verbs add *es* with *he*, *she*, *it*:
She teaches   he finishes   she relaxes

nouns add *es* in the plural:
bus buses   dish dishes   church churches

With a final *consonant + y*

verbs add *ies* with *he*, *she*, *it*:
I hurry he hurries I study she studies

nouns add *ies* in the plural:
hobby hobbies lady ladies

Note
He, she, it *goes*
potato potato*es*

Irregular noun plurals

The plural of most nouns is: *noun + s*
name names day days week weeks

The plural of some nouns is irregular:

man	men	child	children
woman	women	tooth	teeth

Note
The word *police* is plural. Say *the police are*, *the police have*, etc.
The police here are helpful.
The police here haven't got guns.

Possession

We add *'s*

to singular nouns (persons and animals)
Steve's parents
the dog's tail

to irregular noun plurals
women's magazines
children's toys

We add ' to plural nouns (persons and animals)

their parents' house
the neighbours' dog

The indefinite article

A, *an* mean *every*, *each* in:
Jill teaches five hours *a day*.
She goes to a supermarket twice *a week*.
Jill's bus goes three times *an hour*.

Exercise 44

Give the correct form of the verb or noun.

Jill (hurry) to work. — Jill *hurries* to work.
Steve has got two (hobby). — Steve has got two *hobbies*.

Jill has got fourteen (student) in her class, seven (man) and seven (woman). They are of different (nationality). Some are married and have got small (child). Yasuko (study) English at one of the (university) in Japan. Astrid and Maurice (study) English, too. Luisa is an air hostess. She (fly) to many different (country).

Exercise 45

Give the correct form of the verb or noun.

Jill starts work at 9 o'clock three days a week. She usually (catch) the 8.30 bus, but she sometimes (miss) it. It sometimes (pass) her on the way to the bus stop. The (bus) are often full, so they (pass) the bus stop and don't stop. She gets off the bus in Oxford Street, (cross) the street and (rush) to the school. She is seldom late for her 9 o'clock (class).

Exercise 46

Complete with *brother*, *daughter-in-law*, *father*, *grandmother*, *mother*, *nephew*, *parents*, *son*, *uncle*, *wife*.

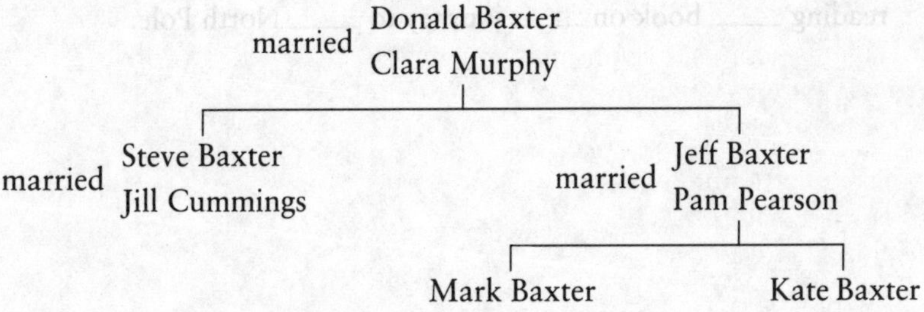

Jeff – Steve: *Jeff is Steve's brother.*

Clara Baxter – the children: *Clara Baxter is the children's grandmother.*

1 Pam – Jeff
2 Steve – the children
3 Jill – Donald Baxter
4 Donald and Clara Baxter – Steve
5 Steve and Jeff – Donald Baxter
6 Jeff – Kate
7 Mark – Steve
8 Clara Baxter – Jeff

Exercise 47

Rewrite, as in the examples.

The house belongs to my parents. *It's my parents' house.*
The books belong to Enrico. *They are Enrico's books.*

1 The flat belongs to the Baxters.
2 The photographs belong to Jill.
3 The house belongs to our friends.
4 The ball belongs to the children.
5 The dog belongs to our neighbour.
6 The coat belongs to Jill.
7 The children belong to our neighbours.
8 The money belongs to my relations.
9 The typewriter belongs to Steve.
10 The books belong to the students.

Exercise 48

Complete with *a*, *an*, *the*.

1 Jill teaches five hours ____ day. During ____ week she doesn't go to ____ restaurant, but at ____ weekend she and Steve sometimes go out.
2 Jill catches ____ bus home, but ____ buses are sometimes full, so she takes ____ Underground. Jill's bus goes three times ____ hour.
3 In ____ evening, Jill reads ____ women's magazine. Now she is reading ____ book on ____ journey to ____ North Pole.

10 Question words How much, how many How often

An interview with a football player

Steve What time does your day start, Sam?
Sam Oh, that's an easy question! Late! Never before 10 o'clock.
Steve And when do you train with the team?
Sam Five days a week. Not on Saturdays or Sundays.
Steve And how many hours do you train every day?
Sam About four hours a day. It's hard work.
Steve And how often do you travel abroad?
Sam Oh, once a month, sometimes twice a month.
Steve What do you do in your free time?
Sam I drive my sports car. I visit my girlfriends . . .
Steve Expensive hobbies! Er . . . how much do you earn?
Sam A lot. Oh, in my free time I read all my fan letters, of course. I get hundreds of letters a week.
Steve And how do you answer all of them?
Sam I don't. I answer letters once a year, at Christmas.
Steve Why do people like you?
Sam Er . . . that's a difficult question. Read my fan letters. Here they are.

Question words with do

Question word	auxiliary	subject	verb	object	adverb phrase
What	do	you	do		in your free time?
When	do	you	train		with the team?
Where	does	Sam	train		with the team?
Why	do	girls	like	you	so much?
How	do	you	answer	them?	

How much, how many

How much + singular noun
How much money do you earn?

How many + plural noun
How many letters do you get a week?

How much, *how many* also stand alone when the meaning is clear:
How much do you earn?
How many (letters) do you get a week?

How often

How often do you train?	I train once a week.
How often do you play golf?	I play golf twice a week.
How often do you go shopping?	I go shopping three times a week.

Exercise 49

Steve asks:

where Sam trains *Where do you train?*

1 what he does on Sundays
2 where he spends his holidays
3 why he likes football
4 how he spends his money
5 where he plays golf
6 what he does in the evenings
7 how often he watches football on television
8 how much he earns
9 what he does on holiday
10 what time he goes to bed

Exercise 50

How much, how many.

1 _____ hours does Sam train every day?
2 _____ fan letters does he get a week?
3 _____ money does he spend on clothes?
4 _____ cars has he got?
5 _____ beer does he drink a day?
6 _____ parties does he go to?
7 _____ time does he spend on other sports?
8 _____ interviews does he give?
9 _____ fans has he got?
10 _____ friends has he got?

Exercise 51

Answer these questions.

How often does Sam play golf? (2, week)
He plays golf *twice a week*.

1 How often does Sam train? (5, week)
2 How often does he go on holiday? (3, year)
3 How often does he answer his fan letters? (1, year)
4 How often does he go out with friends? (2, week)
5 How often does he buy a new car? (1, year)
6 How often does he give an interview? (about 2, month)

Exercise 52

Ask and answer questions with *how often*.

Jill, go shopping? (2)
How often does Jill go shopping? *Twice a week.*

Sam, you train with the team? (5)
Sam, how often do you train with the team? *Five times a week.*

1 Harry, eat at a restaurant? (3)
2 Jill, phone her mother? (1)
3 Pam, you visit your parents? (2)
4 Steve, meet Jeff? (1)
5 Jill, you start classes at 9 o'clock? (3)
6 Jill and Steve, visit Steve's parents? (1)
7 Sam, play golf? (2)
8 Sam, you go out with your friends? (2)
9 Pam and Jeff, watch television? (4)
10 Jill, wash her hair? (1)

Exercise 53

Complete with a preposition.

1 Sam's day never starts _____ 10 o'clock _____ the morning. He doesn't train _____ the team _____ Saturdays and Sundays. _____ his free time he reads his fan letters, but he doesn't reply _____ them, only _____ Christmas.
2 Jill finishes work _____ about 4 o'clock _____ the afternoon. She doesn't teach _____ Saturdays. _____ supper, she relaxes _____ a book or a magazine, or she watches a film _____ television.

Exercise 54

Monika is buying presents.

Coat	£50.00	
Bag	£12.00	
Sweater	£ 8.00	(buy 3)
Dress	£15.00	
Tie	£ 3.00	(buy 4)
Toy car	£ 0.85	(buy 2)
Record	£ 4.50	(buy 3)

Ask and answer questions with *how much* and *how many.*

How many coats is Monika buying? *She's buying one coat.*
How much does it cost? *It costs £50.00.*

11 Have
Too, enough
Why?

On Fridays

On Fridays, Steve often has lunch with Harry. They have a meal at a restaurant or they have a sandwich at a snack bar. Jill doesn't have lunch until 1.30. After lunch, she has coffee with the other teachers. Steve and Harry sometimes have a drink at a pub. In the evening, Jill and Steve don't have supper until 8 o'clock.

Shopping

Astrid Look, here's a lovely blue coat, but it's too big for me.
Luisa And here's a pretty blouse, but it's too small for me.
Astrid Here's a beautiful red blouse. It's big enough, but I can't buy it because it's too expensive. Look, the black skirt is very nice, too. But I can't buy it.
Luisa Why? It's cheap enough.
Astrid Because it's too short.

Have

I You We They	have	lunch.	Do	I you we they	have . . .?	I You We They	do not (don't)	have . . .
He She	has	lunch.	Does	he she	have . . .?	He She	does not (doesn't)	have . . .

Short forms

There are no short forms. 'He's lunch' is wrong. Say 'He has lunch'.

Short answers

Do you have lunch at 12 o'clock?	Yes, I do.	No, I don't.
Does he have breakfast at 8?	Yes, he does.	No, he doesn't, etc.

Use

Have means	*take*	have a shower, a bath
		have a holiday, have a lesson
	eat	have breakfast, lunch, dinner
		have a meal, a sandwich, a snack
	drink	have a coffee, tea, a drink, a beer
	smoke	have a cigarette
	give	have a party
	invite	have people to dinner
	enjoy	have a good time

Too, enough

be + *too* + adjective
be + adjective + *enough*

The coat is *too big* for Astrid.
The blouse isn't *big enough* for Luisa.

Why . . .? Because . . .

Question: Why . . .?
Answer: Because . . .

Why is she angry? *Because* she can't have a holiday now.
Why can't she buy the blouse? *Because* it's too expensive.

Exercise 55

A typical week.

Mondays	breakfast: 6 o'clock (Jeff) piano lesson (the children)
Tuesdays	morning coffee with the neighbour (Pam) dinner with friends (Pam and Jeff)
Wednesdays	lunch with Jack (Jeff)
Thursdays	tea with Aunt Susan (Pam and the children) drink with Fred at the 'Red Lion' (Jeff)
Fridays	driving lesson (Pam)
Saturdays	friends to dinner (Pam and Jeff)
Sundays	dinner with Pam's parents (Pam, Jeff and the children)

Make sentences, as in the examples.

Jeff has breakfast at 6 on Mondays.
The children have a piano lesson on Mondays.

Exercise 56

See Exercise 55.

Make questions, as in the examples.

Does Jeff have breakfast at 6 on Mondays?
Do the children have a piano lesson on Mondays?

Exercise 57

See Exercise 55.

Make sentences, as in the examples.

Jeff, breakfast, 6, Tuesdays.
Jeff doesn't have breakfast at 6 on Tuesdays.

The children, piano lesson, Fridays.
The children don't have a piano lesson on Fridays.

1 Jeff, lunch, Jack, Tuesdays.
2 Pam, driving lesson, Saturdays.
3 Pam and Jeff, friends to dinner, Sundays.
4 Jeff, a drink, Fred, Mondays.
5 Pam and Jeff, dinner, friends, Sundays.
6 Pam, morning coffee, the neighbour, Saturdays.
7 Pam and the children, tea, Aunt Susan, Mondays.
8 The Baxters, dinner, Pam's parents, Saturdays.

Exercise 58

Monika's notebook:

blue blouse: small
red blouse: expensive
brown sweater: thin
striped tie: dark
grey coat: short
black skirt: short
black jacket: long
leather bag: small
lighter: expensive

Ask and answer questions.

Why can't Monika buy the black skirt?
Because it's too short.

Exercise 59

See Exercise 58.

Monika says:

The black skirt isn't long enough, the blue blouse . . .

Remember:
long – short
big – small
cheap – expensive
thick – thin
dark – light

12 Be: past
Have: past
This, that
Spelling

A visit to Madame Tussaud's

Jill is visiting Madame Tussaud's wax museum with her students.

Luisa Who's this fat man here?
Jill That's King Henry VIII. He was King of England from 1509 to 1547.
Ali And who are the six women with him?
Jill His wives! They were all married to Henry. He had six wives. His first wife was Spanish and . . . oh, but that's a long story.
María And who's that figure over there by the door?
Jill That's Queen Elizabeth I. She was Queen of England from 1558 to 1603. She had a long life.
Yasuko And who were these people here?
Jill They were all famous European politicians.
Luisa And who were those men over there on the right?
Jill They were all famous British politicians.
Astrid And who's this figure here near the exit?
Man I'm the attendant, Miss!

Be: past

I He She It	was	Was	I . . .? he . . .? she . . .? it . . .?	I He She It	was not (wasn't)
We You They	were	Were	we . . .? you . . .? they . . .?	We You They	were not (weren't)

Short answers

Were you at Madame Tussaud's?	Yes, I was.	No, I wasn't.
	Yes, we were.	No, we weren't, etc.

Have: past

I	had	Had	I . . .?	I	had not (hadn't)
You			you . . .?	You	
He			he . . .?	He	
She			she . . .?	She	
It			it . . .?	It	
We			we . . .?	We	
You			you . . .?	You	
They			they . . .?	They	

Demonstratives: this, that

Demonstratives + noun

	Near	Far
Singular	this man	that man
Plural	these men	those men

Often *here*, *there*, and *over there* follow *this*, *that + noun*.

Who's this man here?
Who are those women over there?

Spelling

Some nouns with the ending *-fe* and *-f* change *f* to *v* in the plural.

wife	wives	shelf	shelves
life	lives	half	halves
knife	knives	loaf	loaves

Exercise 60

Was, were, had.

Jill Yesterday I _____ at the wax museum with the students. We _____ there very early, but it _____ full. We _____ an interesting afternoon. The students _____ very interested in the historic figures.
Steve _____ you tired afterwards?
Jill No, we _____. We only _____ time for three rooms.

Exercise 61

Contradict these statements.

You were late for work this morning.
Oh, no, I wasn't!

Your students weren't interested in the exhibition.
Oh, yes, they were!

1 You weren't in school at 9 o'clock this morning.
2 Mr Short was angry with Steve.
3 Pam and Jeff were on holiday in Spain.
4 Where's my newspaper? It was on the table before breakfast.
5 Jill's students were tired after the visit to Madame Tussaud's.
6 I wasn't late home last night.
7 I was early this morning.
8 You were in the bath for over an hour.
9 Pam and Jeff weren't on holiday in July.
10 Astrid was in Jill's picture.

Exercise 62

Ask questions with *was*, *were*.

1 Where, Jill's students?
2 When, Jill's students at Madame Tussaud's?
3 Who, Elizabeth I?
4 What, Henry VIII?
5 Why, European politicians at Madame Tussaud's?
6 Who, the six women?

Exercise 63

Make the sentences plural.

This letter is for Jill.	*These letters are for Jill.*
That book was interesting.	*Those books were interesting.*

1 This magazine was expensive.
2 That man is from Oxford.
3 This newspaper article is interesting.
4 That postcard is for Steve.
5 This dictionary was cheap.
6 This flat is very modern.

Exercise 64

Complete with *this*, *that*, *these*, *those*.

Yasuko Who's ____ woman here? And who are ____ six women over there?
Luisa I'm not sure. But look, ____ man there is Henry VIII.
Yasuko Yes, that's right, and ____ men here were famous politicians.
Monika ____ figures over there on the right were British Prime Ministers.
Pascale Yes, that's right, and ____ figures here on the left are famous sportsmen.

Exercise 65

Make the sentences plural.

This loaf of bread isn't fresh.
These loaves of bread aren't fresh.

1 This shelf is dirty.
2 That knife is very sharp.
3 That child upstairs makes a lot of noise.
4 This lady comes from Oxford.
5 My wife is very busy.
6 Use this dictionary.
7 His life was very interesting. (Begin: Their . . .)
8 This dish was cheap.
9 That loaf of bread was expensive.
10 That man knows Steve.

13 Simple past
The date
Let's

Yesterday we visited Madame Tussaud's

Steve I'm hungry. Let's eat! Let's cook a pizza.

Jill Well, I'm busy now.

Steve What are you doing, Jill?

Jill I'm writing my diary. Today is Tuesday 29th July. Yesterday was Monday 28th. What did I do yesterday? Oh, yes! Of course! We visited Madame Tussaud's yesterday afternoon. The students enjoyed it.

Steve Did they like the historic figures?

Jill Yes, they did. On the way back, Ali wanted to know about King Henry VIII.

Steve Did you visit all the rooms?

Jill No, we didn't. We walked round for almost two hours and finished our visit at 4 o'clock. Unfortunately, it rained on the way back. It didn't stop until 5 o'clock.

Steve Did you get wet?

Jill Yes, of course we did!

Simple past: regular verbs

verb + ed

I You He She It We You They	visit*ed* . . .	Did	I you he she it we you they	visit . . .?

I	did not (didn't)	visit . . .
You		
He		
She		
It		
We		
You		
They		

Short answers

Did you visit Madame Tussaud's yesterday?
Yes, we did. No, we didn't, etc.

Use

For completed actions in the past. Often with *yesterday*, *three weeks ago*, *last year*, *in July*, etc.

I visited a museum yesterday.

Pronunciation of -ed

-ed = /d/	enjoyed rained	
-ed = /t/	walked stopped finished watched	after a final *f, k, p, s, sh, ch*
-ed = /ɪd/	wanted visited	after a final *t, d*

Days of the week

What day is it today? It's Monday.
Tuesday.
Wednesday.
Thursday.
Friday.
Saturday.
Sunday.

Note
On Monday means 'next Monday' or 'last Monday'.
On Mondays means 'every Monday'.

The date

What's the date today?

We write:
It's 1st January (or January 1st).
2nd January
3rd January
4th January
11th, 12th, 13th January
21st, 22nd, 23rd January, etc.

We say:
It's the first of January. (January the first)
the second of . . .
the third of . . .
the fourth of . . .

Let's

We make suggestions with *let's*.
let's = let us.

Affirmative: let's + verb
Let's go out.
Let's cook a pizza.

Negative: let's + not + verb
Let's not go out.
Let's not cook a pizza.

Exercise 66

Give Jill's answers.

Steve Let's invite the Thompsons to supper on Sunday. (last Sunday)
Jill *Oh, no! We invited them to supper last Sunday.*

1 Let's help your father with the garden again. (last weekend)
2 Well, let's ask Harry and Pat to come over. (only a few days ago)
3 I know! Let's visit Uncle Peter. (last month)
4 Let's play cards with Mike and Joan again. (last Saturday evening)
5 Let's wash the car. (last week)
6 Well, let's cook a Chinese meal again on Saturday night. (last Saturday night)
7 I know! Let's visit your Aunt Mary. (about four weeks ago)
8 Well, let's watch television. (the day before yesterday)
OK! Then let's stay at home and do nothing.

Exercise 67

This is Steve's diary. Answer the questions.

Monday 21st	9.00 2.00	visit to BBC Television Centre opening of Trinity Hospital
Tuesday 22nd	10.15 2.15	interview Lord Harley press conference at Heathrow Airport
Wednesday 23rd	9.30	discuss new projects with Mr Short
Thursday 24th	11.00 3.00	interview Sam Jones press conference at Hilton Hotel
Friday 25th	4.00	phone Scotland Yard (Chief Insp. Marks)

Did Steve interview Sam Jones on Wednesday?
No, he didn't. He interviewed him on Thursday morning at 11.00.

When did Steve attend the press conference at the Hilton?
He attended the press conference at the Hilton on Thursday afternoon at 3.00.

1 Did Steve interview Lord Harley on Friday?
2 When did he attend the opening of Trinity Hospital?
3 When did he visit the BBC Television Centre?
4 Did he discuss new projects with Mr Short on Friday morning?
5 When did he attend the press conference at Heathrow Airport?
6 Did he phone Chief Inspector Marks on Friday afternoon?

Exercise 68

Ask questions.

Steve phoned Scotland Yard on Friday. (Why?)
Why did Steve phone Scotland Yard on Friday?

Steve interviewed Sam Jones, the football player. (When?)
When did Steve interview Sam Jones?

1 Steve attended a press conference on Tuesday. (Where?)
2 Steve phoned Scotland Yard. (When?)
3 He discussed new projects with Mr Short on Wednesday. (What?)
4 He phoned Lord Harley's secretary before the interview. (How many times?)

5 He visited the BBC Television Centre on Monday. (At what time?)
6 He interviewed Lord Harley on Tuesday morning. (Why?)

Exercise 69

Ask questions.

Jill often runs for the bus in the mornings. (yesterday morning?)
Did she run for the bus yesterday morning?

Jill and Steve often visit Steve's parents at the weekend. (last weekend?)
Did they visit Steve's parents last weekend?

1 Jill usually goes shopping on Fridays. (last Friday?)
2 Steve often stays in the office till 8 pm. (last night?)
3 Luisa usually enjoys exhibitions. (Madame Tussaud's museum?)
4 Jill usually finishes work at 4 o'clock. (every day last week?)
5 Pam and Jeff sometimes send postcards from their holidays. (from Bordeaux?)
6 Ali always asks a lot of questions. (at the museum?)

Exercise 70

Look at Steve's diary (Exercise 67) and give Steve's answers.

Steve, when did you interview Sam Jones?
That was on Thursday, 24th July. (Remember we say 'the twenty-fourth of July'.)

1 Steve, when did you phone Chief Inspector Marks?
2 And when did you visit the Television Centre?
3 When was the press conference at the Hilton?
4 And when did you interview Lord Harley?
5 When did you discuss the new projects with Mr Short?

Exercise 71

Here's a list of the students' birthdays. Write them as in the examples.

Pascale, 11.3	11th March
María, 1.8	1st August

Ali, 13.1
Halim, 29.9
Chu Wen, 3.10
Annegret, 31.7
Juan, 11.11
Enrico, 12.4
Luisa, 2.2

Mikis, 23.12
Yasuko, 25.8
Monika, 4.5
Maurice, 22.6
Astrid, 1.2

Exercise 72

Match the two lists.

The First World War	end/in 1945
Beethoven	walk on the Moon/in 1969
Napoleon	attack Russia/in 1941
Henry VIII	compose the 'Eroica'/in 1803
Hitler	invade Britain/in 1066
Leonardo	discover America/in 1492
The Second World War	start/in 1914
The Normans	paint 'The Last Supper'/between 1495 and 1498
Two men	rule England from 1509 to 1547
Columbus	die/in 1821

Now write sentences in the past.

14 Present continuous Imperative

A long lunch-hour

Steve I'm going to lunch in a few minutes.

Barbara Oh, are you? You're going early today. It's only 11.30. What time are you coming back?

Steve Well, I'm meeting Jill in town. We're doing some shopping together, but er . . . please don't tell Mr Short!

Barbara No, of course not. What are you doing this afternoon? Aren't you discussing the new series today?

Steve Yes, we are, but not until 3. Harry's coming to the meeting, too. I'm going now. Don't work too hard!

Barbara Enjoy your lunch, don't eat too much. Don't spend too much money and don't come back late for the meeting.

Present continuous

For plans in the near future, with or without an adverb of time.

I'm going to lunch in a few minutes.
We're doing some shopping together.
What are you doing this afternoon?

Imperative

Negative: *don't + verb* for singular and plural.

Please don't tell Mr Short.
Don't spend too much money.

Exercise 73

Monday		Liverpool
Tuesday	10.00 2.00	interview John Miller (Heathrow Airport) see bank manager
Wednesday		Birmingham
Thursday	9.00 2.00	visit Ministry of Transport interview Robert Brewster from National Union of Teachers
Friday	10.00 12.30 4.30	attend new art exhibition at Thorpe Galleries meet Dr Parker for lunch at Grand Hotel see dentist

Jill Look, Steve. Here's an interesting advertisement for a flat in Notting Hill Gate. Let's go and see it. What are you doing next week?

Steve Oh, I've got a very full week, Jill. *On Monday I'm going to Liverpool. On Tuesday at 10 I'm interviewing John Miller at Heathrow Airport . . .*

Continue.

Exercise 74

Present continuous or simple present.

On Monday, Jill (visit) Aunt Mary. She (visit) her once a month.
On Monday, Jill is visiting Aunt Mary. She visits her once a month.

1 On Tuesday, Steve (have lunch) with Dr Walker. He always (eat) with him on Tuesdays.
2 Steve usually (go) to see the dentist once a year. He (go) to see him on Friday.
3 On Saturday, Jill and Steve (play) cards with Mike and Joan. They often (invite) them on Saturdays.
4 Jill and Steve usually (help) Steve's father in the garden on Sundays. They (help) him next Sunday again.
5 On 4th August, Steve (drive) to Leeds. He (go) there twice a month.
6 On 5th August, Steve (meet) Dr Green. He (meet) him twice a year.
7 Harry (travel) to Glasgow once a month. He (go) there tomorrow.
8 Jill and Steve sometimes (wash) the car at the weekend. They (wash) it next weekend.

9 The students (do) an English test once a week. This week, they (do) the test on Friday.
10 Jill (meet) Pam for lunch tomorrow. She (have lunch) with her on Thursdays.

Exercise 75

Barbara is interviewing some people at the railway station. What are they doing in London?

Name	From	
Miss A	Devon	meet her boyfriend
Mr and Mrs B	Essex	do some shopping
Mr C	Scotland	attend a course
Mr D and his son	Hull	go to a football match
Miss E and her boyfriend	Brighton	go on a weekend trip
Mr F	Leeds	go for an interview
Mr and Mrs G	Cambridge	fly to Las Palmas from Heathrow Airport
Mr H	York	do business for his company
Miss J	Sheffield	go to a jazz concert
Mr and Mrs K	Wales	visit friends
Mr L	Oxford	attend a business meeting

Miss A comes from Devon. She's meeting her boyfriend.

Continue.

Exercise 76

Be, drop, eat, forget, lose, open, pay, smoke, spend, talk, wash.

Jill Phone the estate agent, please, Steve. Please _____, it's important.

don't forget

1 Buy some cream cakes, please, but _____ them all on the way back!
2 Here's the shopping list and a ten-pound note. _____ it all!
3 You haven't got much time. _____ to Harry for hours.
4 Put that vase on the table, please. _____ it. It was expensive.
5 This bill is wrong. _____ it.
6 The blue sweater isn't dirty, so _____ it.
7 Look at the clock! It's 8.30. _____ late for work again.
8 Cigarettes are bad for you, so _____.
9 This parcel is for Pam, so _____ it.
10 This is the garage key. _____ it, please.

15 Simple past Past continuous

A visit from Jeff

Jill Hello, Jeff. You're back.
Jeff Yes, I phoned you last night, but you didn't answer.
Jill But we didn't go out.
Jeff Then what were you doing at 7.30 last night?
Jill I don't know. At 8.30 I was watching television.
Steve I heard the phone, but I was cleaning shoes when it rang. I had shoe polish on my hands, so I didn't answer it. I called Jill, but she was drying her hair, so she didn't hear it. Then I was walking to the phone when it stopped.
Jeff Ah, I see. Well, we arrived back yesterday afternoon. We left at 3.30. When we left France, the sun was shining, and when we landed in London, it was raining.
Jill What did you do in Bordeaux?
Jeff Oh, several things. Pam lay in the sun and swam in the sea. We met a lot of nice people and the children learnt some French words. We went on excursions and saw a lot of interesting places. Pam bought some souvenirs, we wrote postcards, took photographs, and the children made new friends. Pam spoke French to the waiters.
Steve Did you like it there, then?
Jeff Oh, I thought it was wonderful! I ate a lot, I drank wine every day, I slept until 10 every morning, and I spent all my money!

Simple past tense: irregular verbs

Affirmative: irregular verbs have a special form in the past.

I	ate . . .	Did	I	eat . . .?	I	did not (didn't)	eat . . .
You			you		You		
He			he		He		
She			she		She		
It			it		It		
We			we		We		
You			you		You		
They			they		They		

Short answers

Did you go out?	Yes, we did.	No, we didn't.
Did he eat too much?	Yes, he did.	No, he didn't.
Did they speak French?	Yes, they did.	No, they didn't.

Here is a list of 20 irregular simple past tense forms:

	past		**past**
buy	bought	meet	met
drink	drank	ring	rang
eat	ate	see	saw
fly	flew	sleep	slept
go	went	speak	spoke
hear	heard	spend	spent
lie	lay	swim	swam
learn	learnt	take	took
leave	left	think	thought
make	made	write	wrote

Past continuous

Past tense of be + verb + ing

I He She	was	waiting.	Was	I he she	waiting?
It	was	raining.	Was	it	raining?
We You They	were	waiting.	Were	we you they	waiting?

I He She	was not (wasn't) waiting.
It	was not (wasn't) raining.
We You They	were not (weren't) waiting.

Use

For actions in progress at a certain time in the past.
What *were* you *doing* at 7.30 last night?
I don't know. At 8.30 I *was watching* television.

For actions in progress when another past action begins.
I *was cleaning* shoes when the telephone *rang*.
When we *left* France, the sun *was shining*.

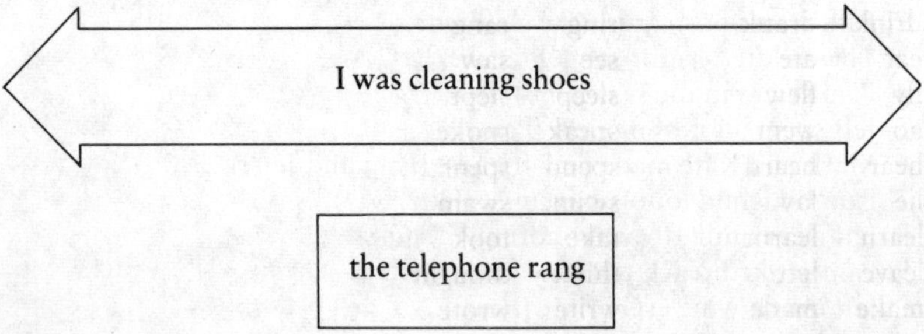
I was cleaning shoes
the telephone rang

Exercise 77

Re-read *A visit from Jeff*. Answer the questions. Use: *buy*, *drink*, *eat*, *go*, *learn*, *leave*, *lie*, *make*, *sleep*, *speak*, *spend*, *swim*.

Did they fly from Bordeaux in the afternoon?
Yes, they left at 3.30.

Did Jeff like the French food?
Yes, he ate a lot.

1 Did Pam understand the waiters?
2 Did Jeff like the French wines?
3 Did Mark and Kate play with other children?
4 Did Pam sunbathe?
5 Did Jeff get enough sleep?
6 Did Pam go in the water?
7 Did Mark and Kate speak French?
8 Did Pam do a lot of shopping?
9 Did Jeff find the holiday very expensive?
10 Did they visit places outside Bordeaux?

Exercise 78

Answer the questions.

Pam lay in the sun all day. (Jeff?)
Did Jeff lie in the sun all day?

Jeff took a lot of photographs. (the children?)
Did the children take a lot of photographs?

1 Jeff ate a lot. (Pam?)
2 Pam wrote postcards. (the children?)
3 The children learnt some French. (Jeff, any?)
4 Pam swam in the sea. (Jeff?)
5 Jeff spent a lot of money. (Pam?)
6 Mark and Kate made new friends. (Pam and Jeff?)
7 Pam bought a lot of souvenirs. (Jeff?)
8 Jeff slept until 10 every morning. (Pam?)
9 Pam spoke French to the waiters. (Jeff?)
10 Jeff drank wine every day. (Pam?)

Exercise 79

Rewrite.

Pam spoke French to the waiters, not English.
Pam didn't speak English to the waiters.

We ate French specialities, not English food.
We didn't eat English food.

1 Pam drank wine on holiday, not beer.
2 We wrote postcards from Bordeaux, not letters.
3 Pam swam in the sea, not in the swimming-pool.
4 We went on excursions by bus, not by taxi.
5 Pam bought souvenirs, not expensive presents.
6 We flew economy class, not first class.
7 We left Bordeaux in the afternoon, not in the evening.
8 I spent a lot of money on good food and good wines, not on presents.
9 We met some French people, not English people. (any)
10 I rang you at 7.30, not at 8.30.

Exercise 80

Give Jill's answers.

Steve Did you ring the dentist yesterday? (estate agent)
Jill *No, I didn't, but I rang the estate agent.*

Steve Did Jeff drink all my whisky last night? (all your gin)
Jill *No, he didn't, but he drank all your gin.*

1 Did you make an appointment for Friday afternoon? (Saturday morning)
2 Did you take that big parcel to the post office? (all the letters)
3 Did you speak to Mr Johnson on the phone? (his secretary)
4 Did Pam ring you at school? (at home)
5 Did you go to the bank? (post office)
6 Did Jeff eat all the cheese last night? (ham)
7 Did you buy any ice-cream from the supermarket? (yogurt)
8 Did you spend a lot of money at the supermarket? (at the new dress-shop)
9 Did Jeff write down the name of their hotel? (two other hotels)
10 Did Pam think the holiday was cheap? (relaxing)

Exercise 81

Look at Steve's diary, page 56.

What was Steve doing on Thursday afternoon at 3.30?
He was attending a press conference at the Hilton Hotel.

1 What was he doing on Monday morning at 9.30?
2 What was he discussing with Mr Short on Wednesday morning at 9.30?
3 Who was he interviewing on Thursday morning?
4 What was he doing on Tuesday at 2.30?
5 What was he doing on Tuesday morning at 10.45?
6 What was he doing on Monday afternoon at 2.15?

Exercise 82

Answer the questions.

1 What was Steve doing when Jeff rang?
2 What was Jill doing when the telephone rang?
3 What was Steve doing when the phone stopped?
4 What was the weather like when Pam and Jeff left France?
5 What was the weather like when they landed at Heathrow Airport?

Exercise 83

Ask questions.

Steve usually cleans his shoes on Saturdays. (when Jeff phoned?)
Was Steve cleaning his shoes when Jeff phoned?

Jill usually washes her hair on Friday evening. (when the phone rang?)
Was Jill washing her hair when the phone rang?

1 Jill usually cooks supper at 7 o'clock. (when Steve got home?)
2 Steve usually washes up after supper. (when Jeff arrived?)
3 Jill usually rushes to the bus stop every morning. (when the bus passed her?)
4 The neighbour's wife plays the piano every evening. (Jeff called?)
5 Steve sometimes drinks coffee with Harry. (when Mr Short called him?)
6 Jill and Steve sometimes watch television. (when the telephone rang?)
7 Steve always reads the newspapers after supper. (when Pam called?)
8 Steve sometimes listens to jazz records. (when the dog next door barked?)
9 Jill does her shopping twice a week. (when you saw her?)
10 It often rains in London. (when the students went to Madame Tussaud's?)

16 Simple future
If clauses

An appointment

Jill and Steve are going to Notting Hill Gate. They are still at home.

Jill Hurry up, Steve, it's 10 o'clock. We'll be late! The appointment is for 10.30!
Steve Damn! We'll never get to Notting Hill Gate in half an hour!
Jill Oh, yes, we will. We'll go in the car. I'll get it. If we leave immediately, we'll get there at the right time.
Steve It'll be quicker if we take the Underground.
Jill No, it won't. Now, where are the car keys? Have you got them?
Steve I hope we'll like the flat.
Jill I'm sure we will.
Steve I expect it'll have some disadvantages.
Jill Where are the car keys?
Steve Well, if you don't find them soon, we won't be there until 11 o'clock! I suppose they'll be in your handbag after all.
Jill Oh, bother! Let's take the Underground.

Simple future

I	will	go.	Will	I	go?	I	will not	go.
You				you		You		
He				he		He		
She				she		She		
It				it		It		
We				we		We		
You				you		You		
They				they		They		

Note
With *I* and *we*, *shall* (affirmative) and *shall not* (negative) are also possible.

Short forms

I'll	go.	I	won't	go.
You'll		You		
He'll		He		
She'll		She		
It'll		It		
We'll		We		
You'll		You		
They'll		They		

Note: with *I* and *we*
I'll = I shall or I will.
We'll = we shall or we will.
I, we shan't = I, we shall not.
'Yes, I'll', etc., is wrong. Say: 'Yes, I will', etc.

Often after *expect*, *hope*, *think*, *know*, *suppose*, *believe*, *be afraid*, *be sure*.
I hope we'll like the flat.
I think it'll have some disadvantages.
I expect they'll be in your handbag.

If clauses

If clause	Main clause
If + simple present	Simple future

If we *leave* now, *we'll get* there at the right time.
If you *don't find* them soon, we *won't be* there until 11 o'clock.

Order

If clause + main clause
or
Main clause + if clause

If we take the Underground, it'll be quicker.
or
It'll be quicker if we take the Underground.

Exercise 84

Use short forms where possible.

Steve Hurry, or we will not get there at the right time.
Jill Yes, we will. We will take the car.
Steve But it will not be quicker.

Jill Yes, it will. It will take about half an hour.
Steve OK. I will get the car.

Exercise 85

Answer the questions.

Do you think the flat will be old or *modern*? (hope)
I hope it'll be modern.

1 Will the estate agent *wait for us* or will he go? (expect)
2 Will it *rain* before we get there or will it stay fine? (be afraid)
3 Will it be near an Underground station, or will it *be far to walk*? (suppose)
4 Will the estate agent be *quite young* or old? (be sure)
5 Will the flat be in a busy street or *in a quiet street*? (hope)
6 Will it be on a bus route, or will it *be far to walk to work*? (expect)
7 Will the rent be high or *low*? (think)
8 Will the flat have *gas heating* or electric central heating? (suppose)
9 Will the block of flats have a lift or will we *walk up*? (be sure)
10 Will our old carpets be all right in this flat or will we *need new ones*? (expect)

Exercise 86

Make sentences with *if*.

Perhaps we won't like the flat. Then we won't take it.
If we don't like the flat, we won't take it.

Perhaps it'll be too small for us. Then we'll stay in this flat.
If it's too small for us, we'll stay in this flat.

1 Perhaps it won't suit us. Then we won't have any problems.
2 Perhaps it will cost too much. Then we won't take it.
3 Perhaps the estate agent will have other suitable flats. Then we'll see them.
4 Perhaps we won't be sure. Then we'll think about it.
5 Perhaps the rent will be too high. Then we'll look at other flats.
6 Perhaps it will suit us perfectly. Then we'll take it immediately.
7 Perhaps the neighbours will have a noisy dog. Then we'll really feel at home there.
8 Perhaps the woman next door will play the piano every day. Then I'll buy a trumpet.
9 Perhaps the neighbours will all be quiet people. Then it'll be ideal.
10 Perhaps we won't find a suitable flat. Then we'll rent a house.
11 Perhaps we won't like the colours. Then we'll decorate it.

12 Perhaps it will have a self-cleaning oven. Then Jill will be very pleased.
13 Perhaps it will be carpeted. Then we won't need new carpets.
14 Perhaps it won't have central heating. Then we won't like it.
15 Perhaps the building will have a lift. Then it will be very convenient.

17 Comparatives

The flat

Estate Agent And here's the kitchen, madam. It's bigger than the average kitchen and modern.

Jill And it's very light and sunny.

Estate Agent And here's the bathroom, with bath, shower, and large wash-basin.

Steve Is it as big as our bathroom, Jill?

Jill No, it isn't as big as our bathroom, but it's nicer. It's a bit smaller, but cosier.

Estate Agent And this is the living-room. Very spacious, big windows, balcony, and a pleasant view.

Jill Oh, yes, I like this room. The windows are bigger than our windows, but the view isn't as pleasant.

Estate Agent And very reasonable at £100 a week, madam.

Jill That's higher than our rent. It's much more expensive.

Steve But it's more reasonable than other flats in this area.

Estate Agent Oh, yes, sir, and the flat's very quiet.

Steve Well, it can't possibly be noisier than our flat, and this is a better area. Well, thank you very much. We'll phone next week and tell you our decision. Goodbye!

Estate Agent Goodbye, sir. Goodbye, madam.

Comparatives

Positive

Affirmative: *as* + adjective + *as*
Jill is as tall as Luisa.

Negative: *not as* + adjective + *as*
or
not so + adjective + *as*
Jill is not as tall as Steve.
or
Steve is not so short as Jill.

Comparative

adjective + *-er* + than
With adjectives of one syllable and with adjectives of two syllables ending in *-y* or *-er*:

high	higher	busy	busier
small	smaller	clever	cleverer

more + adjective + than
With adjectives of three or more syllables:

expensive	more expensive
interesting	more interesting

With adjectives of two syllables ending in *-ful* or *-re*:

useful	more useful
obscure	more obscure

Spelling

sunn*y*	sunn*ier*
eas*y*	eas*ier*

bi*g*	bi*gg*er	thi*n*	thi*nn*er
ho*t*	ho*tt*er	fa*t*	fa*tt*er

Irregular forms: adjectives and adverbs

bad	worse
good	better
far	farther
little	less
much, many	more

The shops here are good, but the shops in your area are better.

Note
Much is used in the negative. Remember: much + singular noun.
I haven't got much time.

Use

We compare two things, persons, or animals.

Exercise 87

Jill and Steve are talking about the flat.

The bathroom wasn't very big. — *No, it wasn't as big as our bathroom.*
The kitchen was sunny. — *Yes, it was sunnier than our kitchen.*

1 The living-room was big. (Yes)
2 The study wasn't very cosy. (No)
3 The bedroom was a bit dark. (Yes)
4 The garage wasn't very convenient. (No)
5 The area is attractive. (Yes)
6 The bathroom was small. (Yes)
7 The street below wasn't very noisy. (No)
8 The windows were all big. (Yes)
9 The lift was small. (Yes)
10 The area is good. (Yes)

Exercise 88

Complete.

Steve If we take the flat, you'll be much (*near*) to your school. The bus journey to the office won't be much longer _____ twenty minutes. The area is certainly (*convenient*) for the buses and the Underground.
Jill Yes, the bus connections are (*good*) than from here.
Steve It's a nice flat. I like it, but the view isn't _____ pleasant _____ from our living-room window.
Jill But it's quiet, and that's (*important*) than a good view!
Steve Yes, I agree. Noisy neighbours are (*bad*) than a poor view.

Exercise 89

Make comparisons.

Jill gets up at 7.45. Steve gets up at 8 o'clock. (early)
Jill gets up earlier than Steve.
Steve doesn't get up as early as Jill.

The Notting Hill Gate flat costs £100 a week. The Baxters' flat costs £80 a week. (expensive)
The Notting Hill Gate flat is more expensive than the Baxters' flat.
The Baxters' flat isn't as expensive as the Notting Hill Gate flat.

1 Steve's salary is £800 a month. Jill's salary is £650 a month. (high)
2 Steve's office is 30 minutes away by bus. Jill's school is only 20 minutes away. (far away)
3 The Notting Hill Gate flat has two bedrooms. The Baxters' flat has only one bedroom. (big)

4 Jeff weighs 85 kilos. Steve weighs only 75 kilos. (fat)
5 Pam and Jeff have two holidays a year. Jill and Steve have only one holiday. (many)
6 The rent for Steve's flat is £80 a week. The rent for Jeff's flat is £95 a week. (reasonable)

18 Simple past
Superlatives

Jill's old diary

Jill Look, Steve. Yesterday I found this old diary. It's eight years old. 1979, the year before we got engaged.

Steve I remember. I paid a fortune for the engagement ring! It cost £90. I spent all my savings on it. Did you read the diary?

Jill Yes, I read it all. 1979 was a bad year for me. Listen! On 2nd January I fell down and broke my arm. Two months later, in March, I caught flu and was ill for weeks. In June I had a meal at a restaurant and was sick for days. Then in July, I drove to Scotland with my sister and a man stole our car. My parents gave me a watch for my birthday and I lost it two days later. I didn't have a good time that year.

Steve But in December you met me at a college party.

Jill Yes, Steve, 1979 was a very bad year for me...

Students' chat

Maurice Is Arabic a difficult language, Halim?

Halim Well, not for me. I think Chinese is one of the most difficult languages for Europeans.

Maurice Yes, I think Spanish and Italian are two of the easiest, and nicest, but of course I speak French.

Halim Well, at the moment, English is the most important language for us. And it's certainly the most useful.

Juan It was always my worst subject at school.

Halim It was never my best subject, that's why I studied engineering.

Have: past

I	had a drink.	Did	I	have . . .?	I	did not (didn't)	have . . .
You			you		You		
He			he		He		
She			she		She		
It			it		It		
We			we		We		
You			you		You		
They			they		They		

Short answers

Did you have a drink? Yes, I did. No, I didn't, etc.

Use

When *have* means *take*, *eat*, *drink*, *smoke*, *give*, *invite*, *enjoy*, we use *did . . . have* for questions and *did not have* for negatives in the past.

Simple past: irregular verbs

	past		past
break	broke	give	gave
catch	caught	lose	lost
cost	cost	meet	met
drive	drove	pay	paid
fall	fell	read	read/red/
feel	felt	say	said
find	found	spend	spent
get	got	steal	stole

Superlative

adjective + *-est*
With adjectives of one syllable and with adjectives of two syllables ending in *-y* or *-er*:

big	bigger	the biggest
busy	busier	the busiest

most + adjective
With adjectives of three or more syllables:

expensive	more expensive	the most expensive
interesting	more interesting	the most interesting

With adjectives of two syllables ending in *-ful* or *-re*:

careful	more careful	the most careful
obscure	more obscure	the most obscure

With some adjectives of two syllables, we can have:

common	commoner	commonest
common	more common	the most common

Use

We compare three or more things, persons, or animals.

Irregular forms: adjectives and adverbs

bad	worse	the worst
good	better	the best
far	farther	the farthest
little	less	the least
much, many	more	the most

The red coat costs £100.	It is very *expensive*.
The blue coat costs £80.	It is *less expensive than* the red coat.
The black coat costs £50.	It is *the least expensive of* the three.

Exercise 90

Answer the questions.

What did Jill find?
She found an old diary.

When did Jill and Steve get engaged?
They got engaged in 1980.

1 How much did the ring cost?
2 When did Jill break her arm?
3 How did she break it?
4 When did she catch flu?
5 Where did Jill drive to in July?
6 What happened there?
7 What did Jill's parents give her for her birthday?
8 What happened to the present?
9 Where did Jill meet Steve?
10 What did Jill say about the year 1979?

Exercise 91

Complete with *buy*, *catch*, *drink*, *drive*, *eat*, *fly*, *go*, *leave*, *pay*, *see*, *sleep*, *spend*, *steal*, *take*.

A thief ____ bracelets and rings worth £1,000 from Mrs R. Abingdon, of 25 Kay Street, Glasgow. He then ____ to a very expensive restaurant, ____ a lot, ____ champagne, and ____ £50 for the meal. He ____ to Edinburgh, ____ his car at the airport and ____ the plane to London. He ____ at his girlfriend's house that night and the next morning ____ a plane ticket and ____ to Paris. There he ____ all the money in a few days. The police first ____ him near Paris, but ____ him in the south of France.

Exercise 92

Use a form of *have* in the past.

Monika Yesterday we _____ a good time.
Jill What did you do?
Monika We went to Enrico's and we _____ dinner there.
Jill What you _____?
Monika An excellent meal. He cooked an Italian meal.
Jill _____ a drink first?
Monika Yes, we went to a pub first and then to Enrico's.
Jill _____ coffee later?
Monika No, I _____, but María and Juan _____.

Exercise 93

There are many old restaurants in London, but this is _____.
the oldest

Mikis Where are the (nice) restaurants in London?
Jill Well, there are a lot of good places. The (expensive) restaurants are in the West End, and the (cheap) places are the snack-bars, of course. And the (quick) places to eat are the self-service restaurants. If you like foreign food, try the restaurants in Soho. You'll find some of the (reasonable) and some of the (cosy) places there, and some of the (tasty) food.
Mikis But where can I find the (typical) English food?
Jill Well, try the fish and chip shops.

Exercise 94

Complete, as in the example.

Jill's students are all over 25, except Yasuko. She's only 23. So Yasuko is _____ student.
the youngest

1 Deng Chu Wen is 34 years old. All the other students are under 32. So Deng Chu Wen is _____ student.
2 They are all intelligent, but who is _____?
3 And they are all nice. Who is _____?
4 They all have good pronunciation. Who has _____ pronunciation?
5 They are all enthusiastic about London, but who is _____?
6 They are all careful students, but who is _____?

Exercise 95

A	B	C	D
£70,000 1910 5 bedrooms garden	£35,000 1900 3 bedrooms no garden	£25,000 1930 1 bedroom garden	£50,000 1950 4 bedrooms garden

John My house isn't the oldest. It wasn't as cheap as Charles's. It is older than Matthew's.
Thomas My house was the cheapest, but it isn't as old as John's.
Charles My house has no garden.
Matthew My house was cheaper than John's, but more expensive than Thomas's.

Complete.

1 A is _____ house.
2 B is _____ house.
3 C is _____ house.
4 D is _____ house.
5 Matthew's house is _____ than Charles's, but _____ than John's. It's got four bedrooms.
6 Thomas's house was _____. It cost £25,000. It is also _____. It's got one bedroom.
7 John's house is _____ than Thomas's, but _____ than Charles's.
8 John's house was _____. It cost £70,000.

19 Possessive pronouns
Be: present perfect

After classes

Jill Whose book is this? Is it yours, María?
María No, it isn't mine. I think it is Halim's.
Halim No, it isn't mine. Ask Maurice. I think it's his.
Maurice Oh, no, it isn't mine. Ask Pascale. Perhaps it's hers.
Pascale Yes, it's mine. Well, not mine, but it belongs to a friend of mine. Thank you.

Weekend plans

Enrico Have you been to England before?
Juan Yes, I have.
Enrico Have you ever been to Oxford?
Juan No, I've never been there.
Enrico I've been there three times. It's beautiful.
Juan Well, let's go to Oxford next weekend.

Possessive pronouns

I	mine	We	ours
You	yours	You	yours
He	his	They	theirs
She	hers		

Whose coat is this? It's mine.
Whose coats are these? They're hers.

Is this book Halim's? Yes, it's his.
Are these books María's? Yes, they're hers.

He is a friend of mine.
She is a colleague of yours.

Present perfect: be

have/has + been

I You We They	have	been there.	Have	I you we they	been . . .?	I You We They	have not . . .
He She It	has	been there.	Has	he she it	been . . .?	He She It	has not . . .

Short forms

I've You've We've They've	been . . .	I You We They	haven't	been . . .
He's She's It's		He She It	hasn't	been . . .

Short answers

Have you been there?	Yes, I have.	No, I haven't.
Has he been to Oxford?	Yes, he has.	No, he hasn't, etc.

Use

He's been to the cinema: he was at the cinema and is back now.

Note

Have you *ever* been to Cambridge?

Yes, I have. I've been there *once/twice*, etc.

No, I haven't. I've *never* been there.

Exercise 96

Answer, as in the examples.

Are these books yours, María? *Yes, they're mine.*

Whose book is this? (Juan) *It's his.*

1 Whose papers are these? (María and Luisa)
2 Is this pen Ali's?
3 Juan and Enrico, are these exercise-books yours?
4 Is this note-pad Annegret's?

5 Monika and Yasuko, are these things yours?
6 Whose pencil is this? (Deng Chu Wen)
7 Are those files Pascale's?
8 Whose folders are these? (Juan and Maurice)
9 Is this ruler yours, Mikis?
10 Is that rubber Monika's?
11 Are those books Juan's?
12 Is that dictionary Annegret's?

Exercise 97

Complete the sentences.

Jill, this is Harry, a colleague ____. *of mine*
Barbara, this is Alison Brown, an old friend ____. *of ours*

1 Who's the nice man with you, Jill? Is he a student ____?
2 Jill, this is Barbara Robson, a colleague ____.
3 Who's the pretty girl with Jill? Is she a student ____?
4 Who are the people with Pam and Jeff? Are they friends ____?
5 Does Miss Parker work at your school? Is she a new colleague ____?
6 Steve, these are Mr and Mrs Walker. They live near my parents. They're friends ____.
7 That's Steve Baxter and that's Harry Turner, a good friend ____.
8 This is my wife, Jill, and this is Miss Parker, a colleague ____.

Exercise 98

Name	Yes	No
Maurice	Madrid, Nairobi	Hong Kong, Rome
Luisa	Lisbon, Berlin	Istanbul, Rome
Mikis	Singapore, Cyprus	Tokyo, Stockholm
Astrid	Amsterdam, Mexico	Buenos Aires, Bangkok
Monika	New York, Toronto	Stockholm, Istanbul
Ali	Paris, Rome	Brussels, Tokyo
María	New York, Berlin	Istanbul, Hong Kong

Has Maurice been to Madrid? *Yes, he has.*
Have Luisa and Monika been to Istanbul? *No, they haven't.*

1 Has Mikis been to Singapore?
2 Have Luisa and María been to Berlin?
3 Has Astrid been to Amsterdam?
4 Have Maurice and María been to Hong Kong?
5 Has Ali been to Brussels?
6 Has Astrid been to Buenos Aires?
7 Have Monika and María been to New York?

8 Has Mikis been to Stockholm?
9 Has Astrid been to Mexico?
10 Have Mikis and Ali been to Tokyo?
11 Has Maurice been to Nairobi?
12 Has Monika been to Toronto?
13 Has Mikis been to Cyprus?
14 Have Maurice and Luisa been to Rome?
15 Has Astrid been to Bangkok?

Exercise 99

See Exercise 98.

Have you ever been to Hong Kong, Maurice?
No, I've never been there.

Has Astrid ever been to Buenos Aires?
No, she's never been there.

1 Has Mikis ever been to Stockholm?
2 Have you ever been to Buenos Aires, Astrid?
3 Have Maurice and Luisa ever been to Rome?
4 Has Astrid ever been to Bangkok?
5 Have you ever been to Stockholm, Mikis?
6 Luisa and Monika, have you ever been to Istanbul?
7 Has Ali ever been to Brussels?
8 Have Mikis and Ali ever been to Tokyo?
9 Has Luisa ever been to Rome?
10 Mikis and Monika, have you ever been to Stockholm?

Exercise 100

Name	Place	When
Barbara	Madrid	1975 1979 1986
Harry	Barcelona	1979 1980
Jeff	Edinburgh	1976 1977 1978
	Rome	1979
Jill	Dublin	1978 1980 1982
	Geneva	1987
	Paris	1985 1986
Pam	Edinburgh	1979 1980 1983
	Rome	1985
Steve	Geneva	1981
	Glasgow	1980 1984

Make questions and answer them.

Jill, Paris?
Has Jill ever been to Paris?
Yes, she's been there twice.

1 Steve, Glasgow?
2 Barbara, Paris?
3 Pam and Jeff, Rome?
4 Jill, Dublin?
5 Pam and Jeff, Edinburgh?
6 Jill and Steve, Geneva?
7 Harry, Barcelona?
8 Jill, Madrid?
9 Barbara, Madrid?
10 Pam and Jeff, Barcelona?

20 Present perfect Yet, already, just

A busy day

Jill Hello, Steve. I'm home. It's rather cold in here.
Steve I've turned the heating on. It's getting warm now. I have been very busy so I'm not cold. I've washed all the windows, I've cleaned the flat and I've answered four letters. I've also cleared a lot of papers off my desk, so it looks nice and tidy now. I feel exhausted.
Jill And have you washed the dishes?
Steve I've already washed and dried the dishes. And I've just made a pot of tea. Come and have a cup.
Jill Wonderful! Have you painted the kitchen door?
Steve No, I haven't started with the doors yet.
Jill You've worked really hard, Steve. Congratulations! Oh, Steve . . . I've invited Pam and Jeff for dinner. They're coming tonight and . . . Have you cooked dinner?
Steve No, I haven't.
Jill Oh, good! Your curries are so good, they're better than mine.

Present perfect: regular verbs

have/has + verb + -ed

I We You They	have	cleaned . . .
He She It	has	cleaned . . .

Have	I we you they	cleaned . . .?
Has	he she it	cleaned . . .?

I We You They	have not (haven't)	cleaned . . .
He She It	has not (hasn't)	cleaned . . .

Short answers

Have you cooked?	Yes, I have.	No, I haven't.
Has he cooked?	Yes, he has.	No, he hasn't, etc.

Pronunciation of -ed

-ed = /d/
cleaned, dried, opened, lived

-ed = /t/ after a final *f*, *k*, *p*, *s*, *sh*, *ch*
washed, helped, cooked, watched, typed, passed

-ed = /ɪd/ after a final *t*, *d*
collected, painted, expected, started, landed, wanted

Use

For past actions without a definite time reference:
I've washed all the windows.

With *never*, *ever*, *already*, *yet*:
I've never been to Tokyo.
He's already washed the dishes.

With *just* for actions in the immediate past:
I've just made a pot of tea. Come and have a cup.

For a past action with a result:
I've turned the heating on. It's getting warm now.
I've worked very hard, so I'm not cold.

Already and yet

1 The train hasn't arrived *yet* = The train is not at the station.
2 The train has *already* arrived = The train is at the station now.

Sentences 1 and 2 mean exactly the opposite.

Exercise 101

Jill Don't forget to answer the letters.
Steve *I've already answered them.*

1 Remember to clean your shoes.
2 Don't forget to polish the mirrors.
3 Remember to iron your blue shirt.
4 Don't forget to wash the dishes.
5 Don't forget to phone Dr Ray.
6 Remember to dust the bookshelves.

7 Don't forget to visit your mother.
8 Don't forget to empty the ashtray.
9 Remember to cook the rice.
10 Don't forget to shave.

Exercise 102

Pascale, visit her cousin in Wales
Pascale hasn't visited her cousin in Wales yet.

1 María, look round all the department stores
2 Annegret and Luisa, visit the British Museum
3 Yasuko, walk round Regent's Park
4 Ali and Halim, use the Underground
5 Enrico, post his letters home
6 Maurice, play cricket in England
7 Ali, ask the way
8 Monika and Pascale, answer their letters
9 Chu Wen, watch television in England
10 Juan and María, listen to the radio

Exercise 103

María, receive a letter from home
María has just received a letter from home.

1 Halim, post a letter
2 Luisa and Yasuko, order two coffees
3 Pascale, cook her lunch
4 Ali and Mikis, miss a bus
5 Monika, wash the dishes
6 Chu Wen, answer a letter
7 Maurice and Juan, arrive
8 Annegret, phone her landlady
9 Enrico, receive a card from his mother
10 Jill, correct the students' homework

Exercise 104

In pairs, ask and answer questions.

Have you ever ____ the British Museum?
visited

1 Have you ever ____ to the BBC?
2 Have you ever ____ golf?
3 Have you ever ____ round Hyde Park?
4 Have you ever ____ a cigarette?

5 Have you ever ____ an art gallery?
6 Have you ever ____ the way in English?
7 Have you ever ____ late?
8 Have you ever ____ a telegram?
9 Have you ever ____ an English television programme?
10 Have you ever ____ with an electric typewriter?

Exercise 105

Complete with *arrive*, *bake*, *change*, *clear*, *cross*, *dry*, *paint*, *park*, *repair*, *wash*, *work*.

Jill and Steve *have worked* all day. Jill's students are coming for tea. Jill ____ just ____ a cake. She ____ already ____ and ____ her hair but she ____ ____ her dress yet. Steve ____ just ____ the kitchen door; he ____ already ____ a broken shelf, but he ____ ____ the papers off the table yet.

Jill Hurry up, Steve. Look, Halim and Ali ____ ____. They ____ already ____ their car and they ____ just ____ the street.

21 Present perfect
Have been, have gone

Have you seen 'Cats'?

Jill Have you seen the musical 'Cats'?
Monika Yes, I've seen it. I saw it last week. I went with María.
Jill Have you eaten fish and chips?
Monika Yes, we have. We had some yesterday. We enjoyed them!
Jill And have you bought any presents?
Monika Yes, I have. I've already spent a lot of money. I spent £50 on Saturday.

Where's Ali gone?

Halim Where's Ali gone?
Juan I think he's gone to the library. Oh, there he is. Where have you been, Ali?
Ali I've just been to the bar across the road. Where's Halim gone? I've got a sandwich for him.

Present perfect: irregular verbs

I We You They	have	eaten.	Have	I we you they	eaten?	I We You They	have not (haven't)	eaten.
He She It	has	eaten.	Has	he she it	eaten?	He She It	has not (hasn't)	eaten.

Short answers

Have you seen 'Cats'?	Yes, I have.	No, I haven't.
Has he eaten?	Yes, he has.	No, he hasn't, etc.

Here is a list of 20 irregular past participles.

	past participle		past participle
break	broken	learn	learnt
buy	bought	leave	left
come	come	make	made
do	done	meet	met
drink	drunk	read	read/red/
eat	eaten	see	seen
fly	flown	speak	spoken
go	gone	spend	spent
give	given	take	taken
hear	heard	write	written

Present perfect or simple past

Simple past: for actions with a past time reference.
I saw 'Cats' *last week*.
There is sometimes no time reference, although the sentence refers to a definite time in the past.
I went with María.

Present perfect: for actions with no definite past time reference.
I've seen 'Cats'.
I've spent a lot of money.

Have been or have gone

He has gone to the library: he is at the library.
He has been to the library: he was at the library and is now back.

Exercise 106

Complete with *buy*, *do*, *drink*, *eat*, *fly*, *go*, *learn*, *make*, *read*, *see*, *speak*, *spend*, *take*.

I have just _____ a mistake.
made

1 Have you ever _____ with British Airways?
2 I have _____ The Guardian but not The Times.
3 Have you _____ 'Hamlet'?
4 Monika has _____ a lot of money.
5 Enrico has never _____ fish and chips, but he has _____ English beer.
6 I have _____ a new coat. Do you like it?

7 Halim has _____ to Wales.
8 Ali has _____ some books back to the library.
9 We haven't _____ the exercise yet, but we have _____ the new words.
10 Jill has just _____ to Pam on the telephone.

Exercise 107

Complete with *break*, *come*, *eat*, *give*, *hear*, *leave*, *make*, *meet*, *take*, *write*.

1 Steve has just _____ back from Liverpool.
2 Jill has just _____ a letter to Aunt Margaret.
3 Jeff has just _____ the dog for a walk.
4 Pam has just _____ the beds.
5 Sorry, Jill. I've just _____ a glass vase.
6 Has Harry already _____ the office?
7 Have you _____ the weather report on the radio?
8 Barbara has just _____ her boyfriend at the station.
9 Has Steve _____ all the cream cakes?
10 Have you already _____ the article to Mr Short, Steve?

Exercise 108

Present perfect or simple past.

Mikis I never (be) to Cambridge.
Maurice Oh, I (go) there last summer. I (do) a language course there.
Mikis You ever (be) to Oxford?
Maurice No, but a friend of mine (stay) there for a month two years ago. He (enjoy) it very much.

Exercise 109

Present perfect or simple past.

Jill How's Pam? I (not see) her in town, Jeff.
Jeff Oh, she's fine. She (be) very busy. The children (be) ill. Last week she (start) an office job, only for the summer months. She never (work) in an office before, so it's difficult for her. She only (be) there a week, but she already (learn) a lot about office life.

Exercise 110

Present perfect or simple past.

Harry I (go) to a new Indian restaurant last night with Mary.
Steve To that new place in Marchmont Street?
Harry Yes. You ever (be) there?
Steve No, but Barbara already (be) there twice. She (love) it. She says she never (eat) such delicious Indian food. What you (order)?
Harry I (have) a prawn curry and Mary (try) a Tandoori chicken. They (be) both fantastic.

Exercise 111

Present perfect or simple past.

Barbara I just (see) Mr Short. He's angry because you (not finish) the report on the bank robbery yet.
Steve But I (explain) the reason this morning. The bank manager (not give) me all the details yet.
Barbara I never (do) a report on a bank robbery before. Is it exciting?
Steve I (not write) many. Last year, I only (write) two.
Barbara (Be) there only two bank robberies last year?
Steve No, there (be) more, of course, but Harry usually writes those reports.

Exercise 112

Present perfect or simple past.

Complete with *buy*, *finish*, *give*, *make*, *paint*, *repair*, *take*, *wash*, *write*.

Steve I _____ some letters. Here they are. I _____ the car, too. Now it shines! And I also _____ the broken shelf yesterday.
Jill Good! You _____ with the typewriter now?
Steve Yes. And I _____ the beds after breakfast.
Jill You _____ the kitchen door? Oh, yes, you have. I can smell the paint. By the way, I _____ your suit to the cleaner's last week.
Steve Thank you. Oh, Harry _____ me two theatre tickets for tonight.
Jill Lovely. I _____ a new dress, so I'll wear it for the theatre.

Exercise 113

Been or *gone.*

Monika I can't find Pascale. Where has she ____?
María I think she's ____ to the bank. Oh, here she is now.
Monika Hello. Where have you ____?
Pascale I've ____ to the bank. Where are Annegret and Luisa?
Monika They've ____ to Brighton today. They'll be back this evening.
Juan Hello. We have just ____ to the Tate Gallery. It was very interesting. Enrico has just ____ there, too. We met him at the entrance. Have you already ____ there?
Maurice Hello. Where's Enrico? I'm going to the Tate Gallery with him. Has he ____ here?
Juan No, but you are too late, Maurice. Enrico has already ____ to the Tate.

22 Have to
Adverbs of manner

Why are you taking this course?

Jill Why are you taking this course, María?

María Well, I'm a secretary and I sometimes need English in my job. I can read English well, but I write it badly. I understand it easily, but I can't speak it fluently.

Jill Do you have to write letters in English?

María Not often, but I sometimes have to speak English on the telephone.

Jill Do you have to write English shorthand?

María No, I don't.

Jill Does your boss have to speak English?

María Yes, he does. He has to entertain English and American visitors. But when they speak fast, he can't understand them correctly.

Have to

I We You They	have to	go.
He She It	has to	go.

Do	I we you they	have to	go?
Does	he she it	have to	go?

I We You They	do not (don't)	have to	go.
He She It	does not (doesn't)	have to	go.

Short answers

Do you have to go?	Yes, I do.	No, I don't, etc.
Does he have to go?	Yes, he does.	No, he doesn't, etc.

Use

Have to + verb = obligation.

Adverbs of manner

We add *-ly* to the adjective

fluent	fluently
bad	badly
correct	correctly

Note

good	well
hard	hard
fast	fast

Spelling

y becomes *i* before *-ly*:
easy easily

-le becomes *-ly*:
sensible sensibly

-ic becomes *-ically*:
enthusiastic enthusiastically

Order

subject	verb	object	adverb of manner
She	speaks	English	well.

Exercise 114

Complete with a form of *have to*.

Jill Why are you taking this course?
Halim Well, I'm an engineer. I _____ read technical texts in English and I _____ write reports.
Jill You _____ speak English in your job?
Halim No, I _____ speak a lot of English.
Luisa I often _____ speak English to passengers. We _____ write English, but we _____ understand and speak correctly.

Juan I have a lot of English and American customers.
Jill You _____ write letters?
Juan No, I _____ write letters, but I _____ dictate letters to my secretary in English. She _____ write English shorthand.
Jill She _____ speak English on the telephone?
Juan No, she _____ do that.

Exercise 115

Make questions with *have to*.

Chu Wen, speak English on the telephone?
Does Chu Wen have to speak English on the telephone?

Mikis, you write letters in English?
Mikis, do you have to write letters in English?

1 María, you, write English shorthand?
2 Ali, write reports in English?
3 Luisa and María, read English?
4 Monika, speak to passengers in English?
5 Astrid and Maurice, you, write essays in English?
6 Enrico, read English newspapers?
7 Luisa, speak to colleagues in English?
8 Halim and Chu Wen, write scientific reports in English?
9 Maurice, you, speak to your teachers in English?
10 María's boss, dictate letters in English?

Exercise 116

Use short answers.

Does Halim have to write technical reports in English? (Yes)
Yes, he does.

1 Does María have to write English shorthand? (No)
2 Juan, do you have to dictate letters in English? (Yes)
3 Does Halim have to speak a lot of English in his job? (No)
4 Do Luisa and Monika have to speak English to passengers? (Yes)
5 Does Mikis have to speak English to customers? (Yes)
6 Astrid, do you have to write essays in English? (Yes)
7 Does Enrico have to interview foreigners in English? (Yes)
8 Do Luisa and Pascale have to write reports in English? (No)
9 Chu Wen, do you have to read English newspapers in your job? (No)
10 Maurice and Yasuko, do you have to write technical English? (No)

Exercise 117

Complete with a form of *can* or *have to.*

Jill Why are you taking this course, Chu Wen?
Chu Wen Well, I'm a chemist. I _____ read English texts without difficulty but I _____ speak fluently. I sometimes _____ write technical reports in English.
Jill You _____ speak English?
Chu Wen No, I _____, but I want to learn.
Jill And you, Maurice?
Maurice I'm a student. We _____ write essays on English literature, but we _____ speak English. I _____ work hard because I want to learn and I _____ speak English fluently yet.

Exercise 118

Answer with an adverb.

Halim is an enthusiastic worker. (Juan)
Juan works enthusiastically, too.

1 Ali is a logical thinker. (Halim)
2 Annegret is a sensible worker. (Pascale)
3 Chu Wen is a methodical learner. (Mikis)
4 Enrico is an enthusiastic reader. (María)
5 Juan's pronunciation is very good. (Monika, pronounce)
6 Pascale is a hard worker. (Luisa)
7 Luisa is a fast learner. (Chu Wen and Monika)
8 Chu Wen is a good writer. (Ali)
9 Yasuko is always punctual. (Monika, arrive)
10 Jill is optimistic about her students' ability. (Jill speaks . . .)

Exercise 119

Answer with an adverb.

Is Steve a good writer? *Yes, he writes well.*
Is he a careless driver? *No, he doesn't drive carelessly.*

1 Is Jill a good teacher? Yes, . . .
2 Is she a careful driver, too? Yes, . . .
3 Is Steve a hard worker? Yes, . . .
4 Is Jeff a fast driver? Yes, . . .
5 Is he a nervous driver, too? No, . . .
6 Is Harry a good writer? Yes, . . .
7 Is he a heavy drinker? No, . . .
8 Is Harry sometimes a lazy worker? No, . . .
9 Is Annegret a fluent speaker of English? Yes, . . .

10 Is Juan a slow reader? No, . . .
11 Is Annegret a good interpreter? Yes, . . .
12 And are they all fast learners? Yes, . . .

23 Going to Plurals Who?

A television thriller

Steve What are you going to do now, Jill?
Jill My jeans have got a hole in them. I'm going to sew them. Where's that pair of sharp scissors?
Steve I'm going to watch a film on television. I'll tell you about it. Now, where are my glasses?
Jill And where are those scissors?

(10 minutes later)
Steve It's very exciting! The man's taking a gun out of a drawer. I think he's going to shoot his wife! Oh, no, he isn't. He's putting it in his coat pocket. Now he's going to the telephone. I think he's going to phone the police. Now his wife is . . . Oh, no! The television's broken! Damn! Jill! I'm going to watch the rest of the film next door!

Who's coming with me?

Annegret I'm going to have lunch. Who's coming with me?
Luisa I am.
Juan, Ali And we are, too.
Annegret Who's missing?
Luisa María and Astrid are.
Annegret They're coming now.
Yasuko Who's coming now?
Annegret María and Astrid are.
Luisa Who went with you yesterday?
Annegret Astrid and Pascale did.

Going to

Be + going to + verb expresses a future intention or plan with or without a time phrase.

What are you going to do now?
I'm going to watch a film on television.

Plurals

Glasses, *scissors*, *trousers*, *jeans*, *shorts*, *pyjamas*, *tights*, are always plural and they have a plural verb.

My *jeans have* a hole in them.
Where are my *glasses*? Oh, here they *are*.

A pair of + plural noun
a pair of scissors

The verb is singular.
That pair of scissors *is* sharp.

Who

Who is, who has, who was
Question: who + singular verb
Answer: singular or plural

Who*'s* coming?	Luisa *is*.	Juan and Ali *are*.
Who *has seen* 'Cats'?	Monika *has*.	Monika and María *have*.
Who *was* here yesterday?	I *was*.	We *were*.

Who + simple past
Question: who + past tense of the verb

Who *came* late today?	Astrid *did*.	Astrid and Pascale *did*.

Exercise 120

Here is Steve's diary.

Mon	present for Jeff
Tues	table tennis with Harry
Wed	car to the garage for service
Thurs	flat in Camden Town (6.15)
Fri	birthday card to Uncle Jim
Sat	football match on television
Sun	jazz concert on the radio

On Monday, he's going to buy a present for Jeff.
Continue.

Exercise 121

Say what they aren't going to do.

Jill has washed Steve's shirts (iron)
. . . but she isn't going to iron them.

1 Steve has driven the car out of the garage. (clean)
2 Jill has dusted the bookshelves. (polish)
3 Steve has peeled the potatoes. (cook)
4 Steve has washed the dishes. (dry)
5 Jill and Steve have received an invitation to a reception. (accept)
6 Harry has given Steve some books. (Steve, read)
7 Jill and Steve have seen a flat in New Cross. (take)
8 Jill has bought a new dress. (wear it for school)
9 Jill and Steve have seen a good colour-TV set in a shopwindow. (buy)
10 Steve has bought some cream cakes. (eat, now)

Exercise 122

Here's Jill's list for the dry cleaner's. Use *a pair of* where necessary.

trousers
skirt
jeans
trouser suit
white blouse
white shorts
red sweater
yellow pyjamas
green dress
Bermuda shorts

She's going to take a pair of trousers.
Continue.

Exercise 123

Make questions with *who*.

Juan and Ali are missing.
Who's missing?

Astrid and Luisa went to lunch with Annegret.
Who went to lunch with Annegret?

1 Pascale and Monika are going to the library.
2 Mikis and Ali went to the British Museum.
3 Astrid and Luisa are coming.
4 Annegret's going to lunch.
5 Pascale's gone to Cambridge.
6 Astrid's waiting.
7 María and Monika ate fish and chips yesterday.
8 Yasuko and Monika were here.
9 Maurice visited the Tower yesterday.
10 Juan's been to York.

24 Some and any compounds No and every compounds Uncountables

The missing file

Steve Where's the 'Latin America' file? I've looked for it everywhere, but I can't find it anywhere. I've asked everybody, and nobody knows. Last week, I put it somewhere in my cupboard, and now it's nowhere! I need some information for my report. Mr Short wants it tomorrow, and I haven't made much progress.

Barbara If I see anyone with it, I'll tell you. Don't worry. Somebody has taken it and will bring it back.

Harry I've got some good news for you, Steve. The file is on Mr Short's desk! Mr Short's waiting for you! Here's a bit of advice, go and see him immediately!

Steve Oh, dear! And you call that good news?

Some and any compounds

something	anything
somebody/someone	anybody/anyone
somewhere	anywhere

Some compounds in affirmative sentences.
Somebody has taken it.

Any compounds in questions, negative sentences, and after *if*.
Is there anything on my desk?
I can't find the file anywhere.
If I see anyone with it, I'll tell you.

No and every compounds

nothing	everything
nobody/no one	everybody/everyone
nowhere	everywhere

No compounds after an affirmative verb.
I've eaten nothing all day.
I've seen nobody all day.
It's nowhere.

Uncountable nouns

We cannot count the nouns *information*, *advice*, *progress*, *news*, *furniture*, *homework*, *luggage*, *nonsense*, *rubbish*.

They have a singular verb.
They have no plural.

The information *is* interesting.
Progress *is* slow.
The news *is* good.

They stand with *some* (affirmative) or *no* (negative).
I need *some* information.
I've made *no* progress.

Note: with *a bit of*, *a piece of*, they are countable.
That piece of information is interesting.
Those two pieces of news were good.

Exercise 124

Something, *somebody*, *somewhere*, *anything*, *anybody*, *anywhere*.

1 Steve is looking for ____.
2 He's looking for the 'Latin America' file. He can't find it ____.
3 He put it ____ in his cupboard last week.
4 Has ____ seen it?
5 ____ has taken it and will bring it back.
6 It is ____ in the building, of course.
7 Barbara hasn't seen ____ with it.
8 Does Harry know ____ about it?
9 If you see ____ with it, please tell Steve.
10 Perhaps Mr Short knows ____ about it.

Exercise 125

Something, *somebody*, *somewhere*, *anything*, *anybody*, *anywhere*.

1 **Steve** Did ____ phone this morning?
Jill Yes. ____ phoned at 10 o'clock. A man from the insurance company.

2 **Steve** Is there _____ on television tonight?
Jill Yes, there is _____ about Japan. It will be interesting.
3 **Steve** Was there _____ in the bank?
Jill No, there wasn't _____ there. I was the only customer.
4 **Steve** Where are my cigarettes and my matches? Are they _____ in the kitchen, Jill?
Jill No, they aren't here. I can't see them _____. Perhaps they are _____ in the bedroom. If I find them _____, I'll tell you.
5 **Steve** Did Pam and Jeff enjoy the party?
Jill No, they didn't. They didn't know _____ there, and _____ spilt wine on Pam's dress.

Exercise 126

Nothing, *nobody*, *nowhere*, *everything*, *everybody*, *everywhere*.

1 Harry is a very popular man. _____ likes him.
2 Did anything happen today?
No, _____.
3 I can't find my watch. I've looked for it _____. It's _____!
4 Jeff is very interested in modern art. He knows _____ about it.
5 The questions are too difficult. _____ can answer them.
6 Is _____ OK? I heard a loud noise.
Yes, I dropped some pans.
7 Has _____ arrived?
Yes, all the guests are here now.
8 It's very quiet in the office today. There's _____ here. _____ is on holiday.
9 What's wrong with the car?
_____, but there's no petrol in the tank.
10 Look at the mess on your desk, Steve! There are papers _____!

Exercise 127

Complete with *some* and *any compounds*.

Steve It's Jeff's birthday next week. Can you think of _____ for a present? _____ not too expensive, of course.
Jill A book on modern art. I saw a lot of art books in a bookshop _____ near Covent Garden. _____ in the shop will help you. I'm going shopping now. If I see _____, I'll tell you. Or I'll phone Pam. If _____ knows, she does. Perhaps she can think of _____.

Exercise 128

Complete with *some*, *any*, *no*, and *every compounds*.

Jill _____ is coming this weekend, so let's go out. Let's do _____ on Saturday. We haven't been _____ for a long time. Let's go _____. I'm sure we haven't seen _____ in London.

Steve But we've been almost _____ in London, Jill. I know! Let's go to that new Indian restaurant. _____ at work has been there.

Exercise 129

Complete with *is*, *are*.

1 That _____ good news!
2 The police here _____ helpful.
3 My pair of glasses _____ broken.
4 Don't believe that story. It _____ nonsense.
5 Steve's article _____ a success.
6 That piece of furniture _____ expensive.
7 These scissors _____ sharp.
8 That piece of advice _____ useful.

25 How much, how many? A little, a few Countables and uncountables

How many eggs are there?

Jill How many eggs are there, Steve?
Steve A lot. But there aren't any apples and there are only a few tomatoes.
Jill And milk? How much is there?
Steve There's a lot of milk, but there isn't much butter. There isn't any cream and we've only got a little ice-cream. There's a lot of orange juice, but we need some beer. There are only three cans of lager. We also need some more bars of chocolate. And buy some biscuits, please, and some more of that lovely chocolate cake.
Jill All those things will make you fat, Steve!
Steve Yes, Jill, and happy!

How much, how many?

Countables	Uncountables
How many?	How much?
A lot.	A lot.
A few.	A little.
Not many.	Not much.
There aren't any . . .	There isn't any . . .

How many eggs *are* there?
A lot = a large number.
A few = a small number, perhaps only 2 or 3 eggs.
Not many = not a large number, perhaps 4 or 5 eggs.
There aren't any eggs = no eggs.

How much milk *is* there?
A lot = a large amount.
A little = a small amount.
Not much = not a large amount.
There isn't any milk = no milk.

Countables, uncountables

Countables: we can count them.
one tomato, an egg, three biscuits
We can put them in the plural.
biscuit   biscuits

Uncountables: always singular.
butter, milk, sugar, jam, ham, beer, wine, orange juice
We say:
There is *some* milk in the fridge.
or
a bottle of milk, whisky
a can of beer, lemonade
a packet of tea, soap powder
a jar of jam, honey, coffee
a tube of toothpaste
a tin of soup, meat, fruit
a bar of chocolate, soap
a loaf of bread
a bag of sugar, flour
a carton of cream, yogurt
a pound of bacon, a kilo of meat

Exercise 130

Ask questions with *how much* and *how many*, and answer with *a little*, or *a few*.

Oil?
How much oil is there?   *Only a little.*

Rolls
How many rolls are there?   *Only a few.*

1 Vinegar?	11 Honey?
2 Cocoa?	12 Flour?
3 Sausages?	13 Eggs?
4 Soup?	14 Milk?
5 Onions?	15 Ice-cream?
6 Ham?	16 Biscuits?
7 Lemons?	17 Orange juice?
8 Cheese?	18 Apples?
9 Salt?	19 Beer?
10 Potatoes?	20 Bananas?

Exercise 131

Some, *any*, or *a*/*an*.

Tea?
Yes, we need some tea.

Sugar?
No, we don't need any sugar.

Cauliflower?
Yes, we need a cauliflower.

Shopping list

tea
milk
flour
writing paper
soap
cauliflower
cabbage

1 Rice?
2 Flour?
3 Cabbage?
4 Toothpaste?
5 Soap?
6 Cucumber?
7 Bread?
8 Writing paper?
9 Note-pad?
10 Milk?

Exercise 132

Jill is going to make a shopping list. They've got

enough:	tomatoes, milk, orange juice
not enough:	potatoes, apples, butter, ice-cream, beer
no:	cream, cheese, chocolate, biscuits.

Complete with *much*, *many*, *any*.

Jill We haven't got ____ ice-cream.
much

Jill We haven't got ____ cheese.
any

Jill We don't need ____ orange juice. We haven't got ____ potatoes. I don't need ____ milk. We haven't got ____ biscuits. We haven't got ____ beer. I don't have to buy ____ tomatoes, but we haven't got ____ apples. And we haven't got ____ butter. We haven't got ____ chocolate and we haven't got ____ cream.

Exercise 133

What did Jill buy?
Use suitable phrases, *a packet of*, *half a pound of*, etc.

Savewell Supermarket	
0.21	soap
0.21	soap
0.65	soap powder
0.35	beer
0.35	beer
0.35	beer
0.48	½ lb butter
0.65	toothpaste
0.20	soup
0.20	soup
0.33	cream
0.89	½ lb bacon
1.15	coffee
0.28	chocolate
0.35	chocolate
0.37	bread
0.45	tomato ketchup

She bought *two bars of soap*, *a packet of soap powder . . .*

Continue.

26 One, ones
Relative pronouns

Shopping

Monika Men's sweaters, please.
Shop-assistant Yes, this way, please. Here they are. These ones here are lambswool, those are Shetland wool, and those are cashmere. Which size do you want?
Monika Medium, I think.
Shop-assistant This grey one costs £44.99. This one is lambswool, £21.99. And here's a Shetland one in brown. It costs £15.99.
Pascale And how much is that one over there?
Shop-assistant That one is cashmere, too. All the cashmere ones cost £44.99.
Pascale Which one are you going to buy?
Monika The first one, the grey one. Unfortunately, I always like the most expensive ones.

At a party

Steve Look, that's the man who knows Jeff well. His name's Carver.
Jill And who's the woman who's talking to Mary?
Steve I think she's the woman who works in Mary's office. Be careful, Jill. Don't sit on that chair. It's the one that's wet. I spilt beer on it! I'm going to have some of that food now.
Jill Don't eat too much. Those are all things which will make you fat.
Steve But I like food that makes me fat.

One, ones

One for a singular noun.
Ones for a plural noun.
We use *one*, *ones* not to repeat a noun.

Which sweaters do you like?
I like the grey sweater and those cashmere ones.
(No repetition of the word *sweater*)
One, *ones* come after *the*, *this/that*, *these/those*, *which?* and after *adjectives*.

Relative pronouns: subject

Who, which/that

People *who/(that)* . . .
Things *which/that* . . .

People who . . . is usual.
People that . . . is possible.
Things which and *Things that* . . . are both usual.

That is *the man*. *The man* knows Jeff well.
That is the man *who* knows Jeff well.

Exercise 134

Astrid is choosing a present for her husband. Annegret is making suggestions. Answer as in the examples.

Has he got an electric shaver? (German)
Yes, he's got a German one.

What about sunglasses? (expensive)
He's got some expensive ones.

1 Has he got a pocket calculator? (American)
2 What about gloves? (leather)
3 Has he got a digital watch? (Japanese)
4 What about sweaters? (cashmere)
5 Has he got a nice pen? (English)
6 Has he got a typewriter? (portable)
7 What about a briefcase? (black)
8 What about nice ties? (silk)
9 What about handkerchiefs? (linen)
10 Has he got a camera? (automatic)

Exercise 135

Answer with *one/ones*, as in the example.

Which of these posters do you like? (with the pictures of London)
The one with the pictures of London.

1 Which of these shorts do you like? (white)
2 Which of these shopping-bags do you like? (with the zip fastener)
3 Which of these sunglasses do you like? (big)
4 Which of these gloves do you like? (leather)
5 Which of these ashtrays do you like? (blue)
6 Which of these pyjamas do you like? (cotton)

7 Which of these envelopes do you like? (white)
8 Which of these trousers do you like? (check)
9 Which of these books do you like? (cheaper)
10 Which of these records do you like? (in the red cover)

Exercise 136

Complete with *who* or *that*.

1 I don't like parties ____ finish late.
2 I don't like people ____ talk about their jobs all the evening.
3 Is that the fruit salad ____ is very good?
4 Aren't they the people ____ bought Jeff's old car?
5 That's the man ____ owns the house ____ burnt down last week.
6 Susan doesn't like guests ____ always arrive late.
7 Steve, is this the chair ____ is wet?
8 That's the girl ____ works with Pam.
9 Steve, is that the cheese ____ isn't fresh?
10 That's the person ____ owns the French restaurant ____ has just opened in King's Road.

Exercise 137

Make questions with *who* or *that*.

That vase cost a lot of money.
Is that the vase that cost a lot of money?

That lady works with Pam.
Is that the lady who works with Pam?

1 That chair broke.
2 That man owns the garage round the corner.
3 That girl lives in the flat above Harry's.
4 That man has been to Australia.
5 That picture cost over £3000.
6 That lady went to Pam's party.
7 That man repaired our washing-machine.
8 That woman opened a dress shop in Duke Street.
9 That wine is very strong.
10 That lamp was very expensive.

Exercise 138

Hotels

Bay
300 years old, near Aberdeen. 150 beds. Bed and breakfast from £14. Five course dinner, £9.50.

Owner: Mrs F. McBride

Crown
New hotel, near Plymouth. Only 2 years old. 100 beds. First class accommodation, £21 a night. Three course lunch, £6.50.

Owner: Mr T. Croft

Embassy
Luxury hotel near Brighton. Golf course, heated swimming-pool. Dinner dance on Saturday evenings, £12.50. Bed and continental breakfast from £28.

Manager: Mr L. Lang

Mill House
Guest house in the Lake District. 25 beds. Good walking and fishing. Bed and breakfast £7.50. Full board £72 a week.

Owner: Mrs P. Robbins

White Hart
Motel near Cardiff. Only 1 year old. 60 beds. £12 a night.

Manageress: Mrs C. Hall

Write sentences, as in the examples. Use *be*, *cost*, *have*, *manage*, *offer*, *own*, *serve*.

The Bay is a hotel near Aberdeen that (which) offers bed and breakfast from £14.
The White Hart is a motel near Cardiff that (which) is only 1 year old.
Mrs McBride is the woman who owns the Bay Hotel.

27 Relative pronouns Whose

Pictures

Maurice That's a picture of a friend I met in Wales. This is a girl I knew at school. And this is the car I bought last year. That's a picture of the family I'm going to visit in Edinburgh. And this is a photograph of the girl I'm going to marry!

Who's he?

Steve Here's a list of the guests who were at the party, Jill. Clive Morris.

Jill Who's he?

Steve He's the man whose photograph was in the papers last week. Angela Berry. She's the woman whose book became a bestseller. We both read it. Do you remember?

Jill The next name on the list is Mr Steve Baxter. Who's he?

Steve Oh, don't you know? He's the journalist whose name became famous!

Relative pronouns: object

Who, which/that

People *who* (*that*) I like.
Things *that* I like.

When *who/that* is the object we can omit it.

	subject	verb	object
That is a *friend*.	I	met	the friend in Wales.

That is the friend *that* I met in Wales.
That is the friend I met in Wales.

Whose

People *whose* . . .
There is no pronoun for things.
That's *the woman whose* book became a bestseller.
The house with the red door belongs to the Smiths.

Exercise 139

Steve and Jill are talking about the party.
Complete with *who* or *that*. If possible, omit them.

Jill I hate parties, but that was one of the worst _____ Mary has ever had. There were a lot of people there _____ drank too much, and there were a lot of people _____ I didn't know. I liked the couple _____ own the restaurant, but I didn't like the man _____ was an architect. He talked about his work all the time, and that's one thing _____ really annoys me!
Steve Some of the people were quite exciting!
Jill The most exciting person _____ I saw there was *you*.

Exercise 140

Pascale and Monika are talking about the presents they bought.
Combine the sentences without *who* or *that*, as in the example.

These sunglasses are for my brother. I bought them at John Lewis's.
These sunglasses I bought at John Lewis's are for my brother.

1 The ashtray cost almost £8. I'm going to give it to my mother.
2 That glass vase is very attractive. You bought it at Harrod's.
3 Those red sandals were very comfortable. We saw them at Saxone's.
4 That black handbag was too expensive. I liked it best.
5 These pyjamas are good quality. I got them at Selfridge's.
6 These books were cheap. We bought them at Foyle's.
7 The blue shirt was reasonable. You bought it in Oxford Street.
8 The shopping-bag is very useful. I bought it for my mother.

Exercise 141

Who killed John?

The Weston is an old hotel in Cornwall. Mr Mann, the owner, bought the Weston 10 years ago. Mrs Mann died last year. Somebody killed a man at the Weston Hotel last night. Mr Mann says he heard the shot.

John is a 50 year-old millionaire. His son hates him. His son is married to Jean, a young woman from New Zealand. Jean is staying at the Weston with her husband. John's wife doesn't like John. She is in Paris. John is the victim.

Charles is a 50 year-old doctor. His wife is American. Charles is also staying at the Weston. He says he heard the shot.

Bill is a 60 year-old architect. He always stays at the Weston. Bill and his wife Helen say they heard the shot.

The killer is married. He isn't young. He isn't with his family.

Complete with *who*, *whose*, or *that*. If possible, omit them.

1 Charles is an architect _____ always stays at the Weston.
2 The killer is the person _____ isn't with his family.
3 Mr Mann, Bill, and Charles are the men _____ heard the shot.
4 Mr Mann is the man _____ wife died last year.
5 The Weston is the hotel _____ Mr Mann bought 10 years ago.
6 John is the millionaire _____ son hates him and _____ wife is in Paris.
7 Jean is the young woman _____ comes from New Zealand.
8 John's wife is the woman _____ isn't at the Weston. John is the man _____ she hates.

Exercise 142

Whose or *who's* (= who is, who has).

1 That's the woman _____ been to Australia.
2 That's the man _____ wife died a year ago.
3 That's the woman _____ book was a bestseller.
4 _____ the woman _____ talking to Mrs Finch?
5 And the man _____ just coughing is a racing driver.
6 That's the man _____ daughter married Lord Milton's son.
7 That's the girl _____ picture was in the papers.
8 That's the lady _____ husband is a pilot.
9 _____ the man _____ standing near the door?
10 He's the man _____ car makes a terrible noise.

28 For, since Would like Want to

Housework

Jill I'm going to wash the windows. I haven't washed them for two months.

Steve And I'm going to clean the car. I haven't cleaned it since your birthday.

Jill I'd like to go to the theatre this weekend. We haven't been to the theatre since 'Hamlet'.

Steve And would you like to go to a disco on Saturday? We haven't been to a disco since New Year.

Jill No, I don't want to go to a disco. I'd prefer to go to the cinema. But at the moment I want to do the housework. Would you like to help me?

Steve Not really, I'd like a drink.

For, since

For with a period of time.
For two years, for ages, for six months.

Since with a point of time.
Since your birthday, since Christmas, since July 20th, since Susan came.

I haven't washed the windows *for two months*.
I haven't cleaned the car *since your birthday*.

Would like

I	would like . . .	Would	I	like . . .?
You			you	
He			he	
She			she	
It			it	
We			we	
You			you	
They			they	

I	would not	like . . .
You		
He		
She		
It		
We		
You		
They		

Short forms

I'd	like . . .
You'd	
He'd	
She'd	
We'd	
You'd	
They'd	

I	wouldn't like . . .
You	
He	
She	
It	
We	
You	
They	

Note: A short form for *it* is not usual in the affirmative.

Short answers

Would you like to go to the cinema?
Yes, I would.
No, I wouldn't, etc.

Use

Would like + *to* + *verb* or *would like* + *noun* express a wish or suggestion.

Wish: I'd like to go to the theatre. I'd like a drink.
Suggestion: Would you like to go out?

Want to

Verb + to + infinitive

Common verbs + to + infinitive are:
expect, *hate*, *hope*, *intend*, *like*, *offer*, *plan*, *prefer*, *promise*, *want*.

I expect to hear from him.
I intend to go to Oxford this weekend.
We'd like to go to the cinema.

We are planning to buy a house.
I prefer to go by train.
She wants to learn French.

Exercise 143

Answer with *for* or *since*.

Jill Let's visit Aunt Alice. (Christmas)
We haven't visited her since Christmas.

Steve Let's go to see a good film. (weeks)
We haven't seen a good film for weeks.

1 Let's play tennis. (five years)
2 Let's visit your parents. (May)
3 Let's play cards with Penny and Graham. (weeks)
4 Let's see an opera. ('Tosca')
5 Let's watch television. (last Friday)
6 Let's phone Helen and Jim. (about five weeks)
7 Let's visit an art gallery. (over a year)
8 Let's invite Harry and Mary to dinner. (March)
9 Let's walk round Hyde Park. (years)
10 Let's cook a pizza. (Sally and Bob were here)

Exercise 144

Answer with *for* or *since*.

Jill I'm going to dust the bookshelves. (last month)
I haven't dusted them since last month.

Steve I'm going to clean the car. (three weeks)
I haven't cleaned it for three weeks.

1 I'm going to wash the windows. (five weeks)
2 I'm going to clean my shoes. (Tuesday)
3 I'm going to make a cake. (your birthday)
4 I'm going to cook a curry. (last week)
5 I'm going to paint the bathroom. (three years)
6 I'm going to wash my hair. (over a week)
7 I'm going to water the flowers. (three days)
8 I'm going to buy a suit. (two years)
9 I'm going to iron. (last Friday)
10 I'm going to wash the curtains. (your parents stayed with us)

Exercise 145

Make sentences with *would like to.*

Jill, go to the theatre.
Jill would like to go to the theatre.

I, go to a disco.
I'd like to go to a disco.

1 Jill, go to Scotland.
2 Steve, go to the cinema.
3 I, go skiing.
4 We, go to Paris.
5 Jill and Steve, go to a concert.
6 They, go on holiday.
7 Jill, go swimming.
8 I, go for a drive in the country.
9 Steve, go to an Indian restaurant.
10 We, go for a walk in Hyde Park.

Exercise 146

Make questions with *would you like . . .?*

go for a walk?
Would you like to go for a walk?

a swim?
Would you like a swim?

1 a cup of tea?
2 watch television?
3 a glass of beer?
4 look at this magazine?
5 visit an art gallery?
6 a piece of cake?
7 spend a weekend in Edinburgh?
8 a new coat?
9 listen to the radio?
10 have lunch in town?

Exercise 147

Make sentences with *been* and *for* or *since.*

Jill, go to the theatre ('Private Lives')
She hasn't been to the theatre since 'Private Lives'.

I, go to a disco (ages)
I haven't been to a disco for ages.

1 Jill, go to Scotland, two years.
2 Steve, go to the cinema, he saw 'Dr Zhivago'
3 I, go skiing, the holiday in Austria
4 We, go to Paris, five years
5 Jill and Steve, go to a concert, last autumn
6 They, go on holiday, last summer
7 Jill, go swimming, she went with Pam six weeks ago
8 I, go for a drive in the country, Mary stayed with us
9 Steve, go to an Indian restaurant, four weeks
10 We, go for a walk in Hyde Park, your mother visited us

Exercise 148

Car Rental

	Days						
Car	**1**	**2**	**3**	**4**	**5**	**6**	**7**
Metro	£10	£30	£50	£70	£90	£105	£105
Ford Fiesta	£11	£40	£60	£80	£100	£115	£115
Ford Sierra	£12	£50	£70	£90	£115	£130	£130
Vauxhall	£15	£60	£80	£115	£140	£165	£165
BMW 316	£18	£80	£100	£140	£175	£200	£200
Rolls-Royce	£139	£400	£500	£600	£700	£882	£882

Name	**Arrived**	**Car**
Mr Strong	Friday 6th	Ford Sierra
Mr & Mrs Patten	Wednesday 4th	BMW
Mrs Willis	Thursday 5th	Metro
Mr & Mrs Parker	Sunday 8th	Rolls-Royce
Miss Lane	Tuesday 3rd	Ford Fiesta
Mr Henderson	Saturday 7th	BMW
Mr & Mrs Green	Monday 2nd	Vauxhall
Mr Butcher	Tuesday 5th	Ford Fiesta
Mrs Donovan	Sunday 8th	Ford Sierra
Mr & Mrs Lord	Friday 6th	Vauxhall
Miss Carpenter	Saturday 7th	Metro

It's Monday 9th June today. You're the cashier. Make sentences as in the example.

You've had the car since last Friday, Mr Strong. That's £70, please.
or
You've had the car for 3 days, Mr Strong. That's £70, please.

Exercise 149

Combine the sentences as in the examples.

I haven't heard from my sister. I expect . . .
I expect to hear from my sister.

We have a big meal in the evening. We like . . .
We like to have a big meal in the evening.

1 Steve went by train, not by bus. He prefers . . .
2 Steve will clean the car. He has promised . . .
3 We are going to Stratford on Avon next weekend. We intend . . .
4 We are going to Scotland for a holiday. We are planning . . .
5 I haven't heard from Jeff. I hope . . .
6 Pam is learning German. She wants . . .
7 Harry will help us. He has offered . . .
8 Steve goes for a drink at "The Globe", not "The Moon". He likes . . .
9 Jill will wait for Steve. Jill has promised . . .
10 We haven't had a letter from our parents. We expect . . .

29 Can, may
Give somebody something
Shall I?

May I leave early?

Enrico May I leave early this afternoon, please?
Jill Yes, you may leave now, in fact. We've almost finished our work for today.
María Can I leave now, too, please? I want to go with Enrico. We're going to a lecture at the university.
Jill Yes, of course you can.
Juan Can we all leave early?
Jill No, I'm afraid you can't!

A birthday present

Jill I've bought your mother a birthday present.
Steve Good. Shall we send her a parcel or shall I give her the present this weekend?
Jill As you please. It's a cashmere cardigan. Shall I show you the cardigan?
Steve Yes, please. Oh, it's lovely. How much did it cost?
Jill I'll tell you the truth, a lot of money!

Can, may: permission

Can I/we . . . + verb?
May I/we . . . + verb?

We ask permission with *can* and *may*.
May is more formal.

May I leave now?
Can I leave, too?

We give permission with *Yes, you may* or *Yes, you can*.

We refuse permission with *No, you may not!* (very emphatic) and with *No, you can't* and *No, I'm afraid you can't* (polite), or *No, I'm afraid not* (polite).

Give somebody something

Verb + somebody + something

Jill gave her the present.
Pass me the salt, please.
I asked the policeman the time.
Jill cooked Steve a pizza.

Common verbs + somebody + something:
ask, *bring*, *buy*, *cook*, *give*, *lend*, *make*, *sell*, *send*, *show*, *teach*, *tell*.

Shall

Shall I/we + verb

Suggestions: Shall we watch television?
Offers: Shall I help you?

Exercise 150

Make sentences with *Can I* and *Can we* (*May I*, *may we*).

María and Enrico want to borrow Jill's dictionary.
Can we borrow your dictionary, please?

1 Steve wants to use Harry's phone.
2 Jill wants to borrow Pam's sewing-machine.
3 Juan and Ali want to leave early.
4 Kate and Mark want to stay up late.
5 Mark wants to have another piece of cake.
6 Kate and Mark want to invite some friends to tea.
7 Juan wants to use Ali's pen.
8 María wants to copy Luisa's notes.
9 Annegret and Pascale want to go to the library.
10 Barbara wants to borrow Harry's car.

Exercise 151

Give or refuse permission with *Yes, you can* or No, *I'm afraid you can't*.

Juan wants to eat in class.
Jill *No, I'm afraid you can't.*

1 Monika and Pascale want to use the lab.
2 Enrico wants to leave early.
3 Juan and Maurice want to smoke in class.
4 Mikis and Halim want to go out.
5 Pascale wants to sleep.

6 Ali wants to open a window.
7 Luisa wants to finish her work at home.
8 Chu Wen wants to read a short story.
9 María wants to go to a pub.
10 Monika and Pascale want to go shopping.

Exercise 152

Steve is too fat. This is his diet.

Every day	Once a week	Never
vegetables or salad	potatoes (2)	cakes
150 g meat or 150 g fish	50 g rice	chocolate
milk (1 glass)	bread (1 slice)	cream
tea (2 cups)	50 g cheese	butter
black coffee (2 cups)	eggs (2)	sweets, sugar, jam
1 grapefruit or 1 apple		wine, beer

Steve *Can I have a glass of milk, Jill?*
Jill *Yes, you can have a glass of milk every day.*

Steve *Can I have a slice of bread and butter, Jill?*
Jill *No, I'm afraid you can't. You can have a slice of bread once a week, but you can't have butter.*

1 2 eggs
2 a grapefruit
3 a glass of beer
4 a cup of coffee and a cake
5 an apple
6 a cup of tea with sugar
7 a slice of bread and jam
8 meat, vegetables, and salad
9 a bar of chocolate
10 fish, potatoes, and a glass of wine

Exercise 153

Answer as in the examples.

What does Jill teach the students? (English)
Jill teaches the students English.

What did Pam pass Jeff? (the salt)
Pam passed Jeff the salt.

1 What did Jill buy Steve's mother? (a cardigan)
2 What did you ask the policeman? (the time)

3 What have you sold Jeff? (my old camera)
4 What has Jill made Steve? (a chocolate cake)
5 What did Barbara give Steve? (her address)
6 What did Pam pass Jeff? (a newspaper)
7 What has Jeff lent Steve? (some money)
8 What will Steve send Uncle Bill? (a birthday card)
9 What does Jill tell Steve? (the truth)
10 What did Jill cook Steve? (a pizza)

Exercise 154

Four of Jill's students want to visit famous cities in Britain. Make suggestions with *shall we*, as in the example.

Monika *Shall we go by car?*
Shall we stay at a bed and breakfast?

Name	How	Place	Accommodation
Monika	car	Cambridge	Bed and Breakfast
María	train	Bath	Guest House
Luisa	bus	Oxford	Small hotel/without bath
Enrico	plane	Edinburgh	Big hotel/with bath

Exercise 155

Make offers with *Shall I*.

Steve offers to carry Barbara's shopping-bag.
Shall I carry your shopping-bag?

1 Steve offers to help Barbara.
2 Steve offers to lend Harry his car.
3 Steve offers to repair Barbara's car.
4 Steve offers to drive Harry home.
5 Steve offers to give Harry a five-pound note.

30 Gerund
Want you to

Do you like reading?

Pascale Do you like reading?
Monika Yes, I do. And I like swimming.
Pascale Yes, swimming is fun. I like travelling.
Monika Yes, travelling is exciting. I also enjoy dancing and I love skiing.
Pascale Yes, I agree. Skiing is fantastic!

I want you to go to Liverpool

Mr Short I want you to go to Liverpool, Steve. I'd like you to be there by this evening. I'd like you to go by car, it's quicker, and I'd like Miss Robson to go with you. I don't want her to work too hard, she hasn't been too well. Now I'd like you both to come into my office and I'll tell you about your work there.

Gerund

verb + ing
reading, skiing, working
writing, smoking, driving
travelling, swimming, running

Swimming is fun.
Skiing is fantastic.

I like swimming.
I enjoy skiing.

The gerund comes after certain verbs: *adore*, *dislike*, *enjoy*, *hate*, *like*, *love*.

I hate waiting in queues.
I dislike driving.

Want you to

want + noun/pronoun + to + infinitive
Other verbs: *expect*, *hate*, *like*, *prefer*.

I want you to go to Liverpool.
I'd like Miss Robson to go with you.
I expect you to help her.

Exercise 156

Combine the sentences, as in the example.

I like travelling. It's exciting.
Travelling is exciting.

1 I like swimming. It's fun.
2 I like reading. It's relaxing.
3 I don't like smoking. It's unhealthy.
4 I like cooking. It's interesting.
5 I don't like driving fast. It's dangerous.
6 I don't like shopping. It's boring.
7 I like riding. It's fun.
8 I don't like diving. It's difficult.
9 I like skiing. It's enjoyable.
10 I like dancing. It's fun.

Exercise 157

Make sentences with *enjoy* or *hate*, as in the examples.

Jill *Can you ski, Annegret?*
Annegret *Yes, I enjoy skiing.*

Jill *Can you drive, Monika?*
Monika *No, I hate driving.*

Name	Likes	Dislikes
Monika	ride	drive
Pascale	cook	knit
Annegret	ski	skate
Yasuko	swim	sew
Astrid	dive	paint
Halim	drive	dance

And you?

Exercise 158

Pam wants Jeff and the children to do the housework. Make sentences as in the example.

Pam wash the dishes, Jeff
Pam wants Jeff to wash the dishes.

1 do the shopping, Jeff
2 dust the furniture, Kate
3 clean the shoes, Mark
4 take the dog for a walk, children
5 buy some flowers, Jeff
6 water the plants, Kate
7 make the beds, Jeff
8 feed the fish, Mark
9 dry the dishes, children
10 hoover the carpets, Jeff

Exercise 159

Make sentences, as in the example.

me, wash the dishes
Pam would like me to wash the dishes.

1 you, do the shopping
2 me, dust the furniture
3 him, clean the shoes
4 us, take the dog for a walk
5 you, buy some flowers
6 her, water the plants
7 me, make the beds
8 you, feed the fish
9 us, dry the dishes
10 me, hoover the carpets

Exercise 160

Five students are organizing a party. María is next to Juan. She wants him to do the shopping. Juan is next to a man. Juan wants him to get the records. Luisa is sitting next to two men. She wants Enrico and Maurice to buy the beer. Enrico is next to a man and a woman. He wants the woman to invite the guests. María is on the left. They all want her to make the food.

Complete.
Where are they sitting? _____ _____ _____ _____ _____

1 They all want _____
2 Enrico wants _____
3 María wants _____
4 Juan wants _____
5 Luisa wants _____

Key

1
1 *Is* Jill a teacher? Yes, she *is*. *Are* you a teacher, too, Steve? Oh, no! I *am* a journalist. *Is* that interesting work? Oh, yes! It *is*! 2 *Are* you Jill Baxter? Yes, that *is* right, I *am*.

2
Excuse me, please, but is your name Bill Blake? No, it *isn't*. *I'm* sorry. You *aren't* Bill Blake? No, *I'm not*. Are you Steve Baxter, the journalist? Yes, *that's* right, I am!

3
Hello, is *your* name Blake? No, *it* isn't. *I* am sorry. *My* name's Baxter, Steve Baxter. Oh! (to Jill) But *you* are Mrs Janet Blake! No, sorry. *I* am Jill Baxter, *his* wife. *He* is *my* husband. Oh, so sorry. . .! Hmm! *He* isn't Bill Blake! *His* name's Baxter! And *she* isn't Janet Blake! *Her* name's Jill Baxter!

4
1 No, he isn't. 2 Yes, he is. 3 Yes, it is. 4 No, she isn't. 5 Yes, she is. 6 Yes, he is. 7 No, she isn't. 8 Yes, she is. 9 Yes, it is. 10 Yes, it is. 11 Yes, I am/No, I'm not. 12 Yes, it is/No, it isn't.

5
Hello. *Are* we all here today? No, who *is* missing? Enrico *is* missing and Luisa *is* missing, too. Yes, they *are* late. I hope they *are* not ill. Good morning! Here I *am*. Sorry I *am* late. Oh, that *is* all right. *Are* you both OK?

6
1 Pascale and Monika, what are *your* surnames, please? *Our* surnames are Dubois and Wengli. *We* are from Switzerland. Are *you* married? No, *we* aren't. 2 The students from Switzerland, what are *their* names, Jill? Are *they* both from Geneva? No, *they* aren't.

7

Juan	Spain	Yes
Annegret	Germany	Yes
Pascale	Switzerland	No
María	Mexico	No
Astrid	Sweden	Yes
Monika	Switzerland	No

1 No, they aren't. 2 Yes, we are. 3 No, we aren't. 4 Yes, they are. 5 No, they aren't. 6 Yes, we are. 7 Yes, they are. 8 No, we aren't.

8
1 Brugg? *Where's* that? 2 *Who's* missing? 3 *Where are* Enrico and Luisa? 4 *How are* you? And *how's* your wife? 5 *What's* your name, please?

9
1 Yes, she is. 2 No, it isn't. 3 No, they aren't. 4 No, he isn't. 5 No, she isn't. 6 Yes, they are. 7 Yes, he is. 8 Yes, she is. 9 Yes, it is. 10 No, it isn't. 11 No, we aren't. 12 No, I'm not.

10
Who's missing? Enrico? Yes, Enrico and Luisa are missing. Yes, *they're* late. I hope *they aren't* ill. Good morning. *We're* both late! Sorry! *That's* OK. I'm glad *you're* here now. Are you all right? No, *we aren't*.

11
1 Yes, there is. 2 No, there isn't. 3 Yes, there are. 4 No, there aren't.

5 No, there isn't. 6 Yes, there is. 7 No, there aren't. 8 Yes, there are. 9 Yes, there is. 10 No, there aren't. 11 Yes, there is. 12 Yes, there are. 13 No, there isn't. 14 Yes, there is. 15 No, there aren't.

12

There are two students from Latin America, but *there aren't* any from Venezuela and *there isn't* a student from Argentina this year. *There is* a young lady from Japan, *there are* two from Switzerland and *there is* a student from Greece. *Is there* a student from Italy? Yes, *there is*. *Are there* any students from Norway? No, *there aren't*. Not this year.

13

Are there *any* students from Switzerland in your class, Jill? Yes, there are two, but there aren't *any* from Holland. There are *some* students from Asia this time. There's *one* from Japan, a young lady, and there's *one* from China, a man. There are usually *some* students from Venezuela, but there aren't *any* this time. Are there *any* from South America? Yes, there's *one* from Brazil, a young lady. And are there *any* from France? Yes, there's *one* from France, a man. Are there *any* students from Scandinavia? Yes, there's *one* from Sweden, Astrid. And there are *some* married students. Astrid is married.

14

It *has* got a swimming-pool. And it *has* got a yoga room. Good! They *have* got a yoga class on Wednesdays. They *have* got a French class, but they *haven't* got a Spanish class. Pity! Oh, and look, Steve, they *have* got a photography class, too. Very interesting. But they *haven't* got a gardening class. . . And we *haven't* got a garden. It *hasn't* got table tennis, it *hasn't* got volleyball. . . And you *haven't* got enough time.

15

1 Yes, she has. 2 No, he hasn't. 3 Yes, it has. 4 No, it hasn't. 5 Yes, it has. 6 No, it hasn't. 7 No, they haven't. 8 Yes, he has. 9 No, I haven't/Yes, I have. 10 Yes, I have/No, I haven't.

16

1 Has Maurice got a Renault? 2 Has María got a German car? 3 Has Astrid got a Fiat? 4 Have Maurice and Astrid got a French car? 5 Has Annegret got a Citroën? 6 Have María and Annegret got a Volkswagen?

Solution: María has got a Volkswagen. Maurice has got a Citroën. Annegret has got a Renault. Astrid has got a Citroën.

17

Open your mouth, please, Mr Baxter. And now *say* 'Ah'. *Stay* in bed until Wednesday and *take* this medicine. *Phone* me tomorrow morning, please and *come* and see me on Thursday.

18

Cream the sugar and the butter. *Beat* in the egg. *Mash* the bananas. *Add* the flour. *Put* into a tin and *bake* for 30 minutes. *Cool* and *serve*.

19

I like *him*. Mr Short and Harry Turner help *me* with difficult articles. And Barbara Robson? Do you like *her*? She's new, so I help *her*. I have a nice office now and I share *it* with Barbara. I like *them*. And do they like *you*? They like *me* and Julia. They like *us* very much. We love *it*.

20

1 work 2 share 3 help 4 go 5 visit 6 like, cook 7 know 8 run

21

1 Do you go to bed early? 2 Do Jill and Steve like Chinese food? 3 Do

you share your office? 4 Do the students like English tea? 5 Do we watch television every evening? 6 Do I visit my relations in the country? 7 Do you find much time for sport? 8 Do their friends love Indian food? 9 Do we run for the bus every morning? 10 Do Jill and Steve go out during the week?

22

Do you like it? Yes, *I do*. And *do* you like my new tie? No, *I don't*. But I *don't* like that tie. No, *I don't*. *Do* you like my new shirt? Yes, *I do*. Jill, *do* you want a cup of tea? No, *I don't*, thanks.

23

1 We eat at a restaurant at the weekend. 2 We enjoy Chinese food very much. 3 We cook it at home. 4 We visit our relations in the country on Sundays. 5 We go to our favourite pub on Saturday evenings.

24

1 a 2 an 3 a, an 4 an, an 5 an 6 an, a 7 a, a 8 an 9 an 10 an

25

1 He's an architect. 2 She's an art teacher. 3 He's a journalist. 4 I'm an engineer. 5 They are students. 6 I'm a travel guide. 7 He's a businessman. 8 I'm a secretary.

26

Deng Chu Wen *works* in Peking. And Mikis *designs* houses in Athens. And Enrico *exports* antiques, María *speaks* four languages and Maurice *writes* for an Italian newspaper.

27

1 Monika 2 Maurice 3 Luisa 4 Chu Wen 5 Juan 6 Pascale 7 Yasuko 8 Mikis

1 No, she doesn't. 2 Yes, he does. 3 No, he doesn't. 4 Yes, she does. 5 No, she doesn't. 6 Yes, he does. 7 Yes, she does. 8 No, he doesn't. 9 Yes, he does. 10 No, she doesn't. 11 No, he doesn't. 12 Yes, she does. 13 Yes, he does. 14 No, he doesn't. 15 Yes, she does. 16 Yes, it does.

28

1 Do they like English coffee, too? 2 Does he read The Guardian, too? 3 Do they speak other languages, too? 4 Do you like the English weather, too? 5 Does he cook Indian food, too? 6 Do they get up early, too? 7 Do you visit friends during the week, too? 8 Do they run for the bus every evening, too? 9 Does he drink whisky, too? 10 Do you like English beer, too?

29

1 of, in 2 over 3 for 4 of 5 in

30

1 Yes, that's my book. 2 Yes, those are my postcards. 3 Yes, that's my briefcase. 4 Yes, those are my keys. 5 Yes, those are my cigarettes. 6 Yes, that's my newspaper. 7 Yes, those are my pencils. 8 Yes, that's my bag. 9 Yes, those are my magazines. 10 Yes, that's my umbrella.

31

1 This is my book and that's your book. 2 These are my postcards and those are your postcards. 3 This is my dictionary and that's your dictionary. 4 These are my stamps and those are your stamps. 5 This is my rubber and that's your rubber. 6 These are my envelopes and those are your envelopes. 7 This is my notebook and that's your notebook. 8 This is my pen and that's your pen. 9 This is my ruler and that's your ruler. 10 These are my cigarettes and those are your cigarettes.

32

1 Jill always goes to work by bus. 2 Jill often gets the 8.30 bus. 3 She is seldom late for school. 4 Jill and Steve don't usually say much at

breakfast. 5 Steve usually goes by bus, too. 6 He sometimes takes the Underground. 7 He always reads a newspaper on the bus. 8 Jill never reads on the bus. 9 Steve usually buys The Times. 10 He doesn't often read at the breakfast table. 11 Steve is sometimes late for work. 12 Jill and Steve are always in a hurry.

33

1 The newspaper is old. 2 The postcards are all from Spain. 3 The felt pen is black. 4 The magazine is for Harry. 5 The parcels are from Aunt Susan.

34

1 Maurice is seldom late. 2 Pascale is often late. 3 Luisa is sometimes late. 4 Mikis is often absent. 5 Halim is never absent. 6 María is seldom absent. 7 Astrid is never late. 8 Juan is seldom absent. 9 Yasuko is always present. 10 Enrico is often late. 11 Annegret is sometimes absent. 12 Monika is never absent.

35

The weather is terrible here, at home *the* sun shines every day. Yes, in Mexico *the* weather is very good, too, and *the* sky is blue. Yes, *the* houses in our street are very nice, but it is noisy. *The* boys next door are very noisy. Well, ( ) boys often are. I live with *a* family. Tom is *a* doctor, and as you know, ( ) doctors are very busy people. His wife, Mary, is *a* teacher. In January they go to *the* South Pole. Now at *a* hotel. But ( ) hotels are very expensive.

36

1 They are spending a wonderful holiday in Bordeaux. 2 Pam's swimming in the pool. 3 The children are playing. 4 Jeff's thinking about Jill and Steve at home. 5 Jeff's drinking a lovely cool beer. 6 Pascale and Yasuko are playing tennis.

37

1 Yes, he is. 2 No, she isn't. 3 No, he isn't. 4 No, they aren't. 5 Yes, they are. 6 No, it isn't. 7 No, they aren't. 8 Yes, she is.

38

1 What's Jeff doing at the moment? He's drinking a beer. 2 What's Pam doing now? She's swimming in the sea. 3 What are the children doing at the moment? They're playing. 4 What's Harry doing at the moment? He's travelling. 5 What's Barbara Robson doing now? She's typing an article. 6 What's Mr Short doing at the moment? He's sitting in his office. 7 What are Harry and Steve doing at the moment? They're wasting time. 8 What's Jill doing now? She's planning lessons. 9 What are the students doing at the moment? They're writing a test. 10 What are you doing at the moment? I'm practising the present continuous.

39

Can you play a musical instrument? No, I *can't*, but my wife *can*. She *can* play the piano. *Can* she play jazz, too? No, but my two brothers *can*. They *can't* play classical music.

40

1 Can Annegret speak Spanish? She can't speak Spanish, but she can speak Russian. 2 Can Deng Chu Wen speak Japanese? He can't speak Japanese, but he can speak French. 3 Can Astrid speak Danish? She can't speak Danish, but she can speak German. 4 Can Monika speak Spanish? She can't speak Spanish, but she can speak French and Italian. 5 Can Maurice speak Italian? He can't speak Italian, but he can speak Spanish. 6 Can Halim speak German? He can't speak German, but he can speak French. 7 Can Luisa speak Italian? She can't speak Italian, but she can speak Spanish. 8 Can Juan speak Chinese? He can't

speak Chinese, but he can speak Italian.

41
It's wonderful here *in* Bordeaux. We're thinking *about* you *at* home *in* London. *At* the moment, Pam's *in* the swimming-pool, and I'm relaxing *at* the hotel bar *with* a glass *of* beer.

42
What *are* you *doing* at the moment? I'*m washing* my hair. You usually *wash* your hair on Fridays. *Are* you *washing* your hair now? No, now I'*m drying* it. What *are* you *doing*? I'*m cleaning* the shoes. But you usually *clean* them on Saturdays. The phone *is ringing*. What *are* you *saying*, darling? The phone *is ringing*! It *isn't ringing*!

43
I'*m phoning* from the office. I know it's late, but I'*m working* now. You never *stay* so late! I'*m having* difficulty with the article on the rail strike. But you seldom *have* difficulty with the articles. You always *finish* them quickly. Steve, what *are* you *doing* just now? *Are* you *watching* television at the moment? Jill *is preparing* lessons for tomorrow, and I'*m getting* ready for bed.

44
Jill has got fourteen *students* in her class, seven *men* and seven *women*. They are of different *nationalities*. Some are married and have got small children. Yasuko *studies* English at one of the *universities* in Japan. Astrid and Maurice *study* English, too. Luisa is an air hostess. She *flies* to many different *countries*.

45
She usually *catches* the 8.30 bus, but she sometimes *misses* it. It sometimes *passes* her on the way to the bus stop. The *buses* are often full, so they *pass* the bus stop and don't stop. She gets off the bus in Oxford Street, *crosses* the street and *rushes* to school. She is seldom late for her 9 o'clock *classes*.

46
1 Pam is Jeff's wife. 2 Steve is the children's uncle. 3 Jill is Donald Baxter's daughter-in-law. 4 Donald and Clara Baxter are Steve's parents. 5 Steve and Jeff are Donald Baxter's sons. 6 Jeff is Kate's father. 7 Mark is Steve's nephew. 8 Clara Baxter is Jeff's mother.

47
1 It's the Baxters' flat. 2 They are Jill's photographs. 3 It's our friends' house. 4 It's the children's ball. 5 It's our neighbour's dog. 6 It's Jill's coat. 7 They are our neighbours' children. 8 It's my relations' money. 9 It's Steve's typewriter. 10 They are the students' books.

48
1 Jill teaches five hours *a* day. During *the* week she doesn't go to *a* restaurant, but at *the* weekend she and Steve sometimes go out. 2 Jill catches *a* bus home, but *the* buses are sometimes full, so she takes *the* Underground. Jill's bus goes three times *an* hour. 3 In *the* evening, Jill reads *a* women's magazine. Now she is reading *a* book on *a* journey to *the* North Pole.

49
1 What do you do on Sundays? 2 Where do you spend your holidays? 3 Why do you like football? 4 How do you spend your money? 5 Where do you play golf? 6 What do you do in the evenings? 7 How often do you watch football on television? 8 How much do you earn? 9 What do you do on holiday? 10 What time do you go to bed?

50
1 How many 2 How many 3 How much 4 How many 5 How much

6 How many 7 How much 8 How many 9 How many 10 How many

51
1 five times a week 2 three times a year 3 once a year 4 twice a week 5 once a year 6 about twice a month

52
1 How often does Harry eat at a restaurant? Three times a week. 2 How often does Jill phone her mother? Once a week. 3 Pam, how often do you visit your parents? Twice a week. 4 How often does Steve meet Jeff? Once a week. 5 Jill, how often do you start classes at 9 o'clock? Three times a week. 6 How often do Jill and Steve visit Steve's parents? Once a week. 7 How often does Sam play golf? Twice a week. 8 Sam, how often do you go out with your friends? Twice a week. 9 How often do Pam and Jeff watch television? Four times a week. 10 How often does Jill wash her hair? Once a week.

53
1 Sam's day never starts *before* 10 o'clock *in* the morning. He doesn't train *with* the team *on* Saturdays and Sundays. *In* his free time he reads his fan letters, but he doesn't reply *to* them, only *at* Christmas. 2 Jill finishes work *at* about 4 o'clock *in* the afternoon. She doesn't teach *on* Saturdays. *After* supper, she relaxes *with* a book or a magazine, or she watches a film *on* television.

54
1 How many bags is Monika buying? She's buying one bag. How much does it cost? It costs £12.00. 2 How many sweaters is Monika buying? She's buying three sweaters. How much do they cost? They cost £24.00. 3 How many dresses is Monika buying? She's buying one dress. How much does it cost? It costs £15.00. 4 How many ties is Monika buying? She's buying four ties. How much do they cost? They cost £12.00. 5 How many toy cars is Monika buying? She's buying two toy cars. How much do they cost? They cost £1.70. 6 How many records is Monika buying? She's buying three records. How much do they cost? They cost £13.50.

55
1 Pam has morning coffee with the neighbour on Tuesdays. 2 Pam and Jeff have dinner with friends on Tuesdays. 3 Jeff has lunch with Jack on Wednesdays. 4 Pam and the children have tea with Aunt Susan on Thursdays. 5 Jeff has a drink with Fred at the 'Red Lion' on Thursdays. 6 Pam has a driving lesson on Fridays. 7 Pam and Jeff have friends to dinner on Saturdays. 8 Pam, Jeff and the children have dinner with Pam's parents on Sundays.

56
1 Does Pam have morning coffee with the neighbour on Tuesdays? 2 Do Pam and Jeff have dinner with friends on Tuesdays? 3 Does Jeff have lunch with Jack on Wednesdays? 4 Do Pam and the children have tea with Aunt Susan on Thursdays? 5 Does Jeff have a drink with Fred at the 'Red Lion' on Thursdays? 6 Does Pam have a driving lesson on Fridays? 7 Do Pam and Jeff have friends to dinner on Saturdays? 8 Do Pam, Jeff and the children have dinner with Pam's parents on Sundays?

57
1 Jeff doesn't have lunch with Jack on Tuesdays. 2 Pam doesn't have a driving lesson on Saturdays. 3 Pam and Jeff don't have friends to dinner on Sundays. 4 Jeff doesn't have a drink with Fred on Mondays. 5 Pam and Jeff don't have dinner with friends on Sundays. 6 Pam doesn't have morning coffee with the neighbour on Saturdays. 7 Pam and the children don't have tea with Aunt

Susan on Mondays. 8 The Baxters don't have dinner with Pam's parents on Saturdays.

58
1 Why can't Monika buy the blue blouse? Because it's too small. 2 Why can't she buy the red blouse? Because it's too expensive. 3 Why can't she buy the brown sweater? Because it's too thin. 4 Why can't she buy the striped tie? Because it's too dark. 5 Why can't she buy the grey coat? Because it's too short. 6 Why can't she buy the black jacket? Because it's too long. 7 Why can't she buy the leather bag? Because it's too small. 8 Why can't she buy the lighter? Because it's too expensive.

59
1 The blue blouse isn't big enough. 2 The red blouse isn't cheap enough. 3 The brown sweater isn't thick enough. 4 The striped tie isn't light enough. 5 The grey coat isn't long enough. 6 The black jacket isn't short enough. 7 The leather bag isn't big enough. 8 The lighter isn't cheap enough.

60
Yesterday I *was* at the wax museum with the students. We *were* there very early, but it *was* full. We *had* an interesting afternoon. The students *were* very interested in the historic figures. *Were* you tired afterwards? No, we *weren't*. We only *had* time for three rooms.

61
1 Oh, yes, I was! 2 Oh, no, he wasn't! 3 Oh, no, they weren't! 4 Oh, no, it wasn't! 5 Oh, no, they weren't! 6 Oh, yes, you were! 7 Oh, no, you weren't! 8 Oh, no, I wasn't! 9 Oh, yes, they were! 10 Oh, no, she wasn't!

62
1 Where were Jill's students? 2 When were Jill's students at Madame Tussaud's? 3 Who was Elizabeth I? 4 What was Henry VIII? 5 Why were European politicians at Madame Tussaud's? 6 Who were the six women?

63
1 These magazines were expensive. 2 Those men are from Oxford. 3 These newspaper articles are interesting. 4 Those postcards are for Steve. 5 These dictionaries were cheap. 6 These flats are very modern.

64
Who's *this* woman here? And who are *those* six women over there? But look, *that* man there is Henry VIII. Yes, that's right, and *these* men here were famous politicians. *Those* figures over there on the right were British Prime Ministers. Yes, that's right, and *these* figures here on the left are famous sportsmen.

65
1 These shelves are dirty. 2 Those knives are very sharp. 3 Those children upstairs make a lot of noise. 4 These ladies come from Oxford. 5 Our wives are very busy. 6 Use these dictionaries. 7 Their lives were very interesting. 8 These dishes were cheap. 9 Those loaves of bread were expensive. 10 Those men know Steve.

66
1 Oh, no! We helped him with the garden last weekend. 2 Oh, no! We asked them to come over only a few days ago. 3 Oh, no! We visited Uncle Peter last month. 4 Oh, no! We played cards with Mike and Joan last Saturday evening. 5 Oh, no! We washed the car last week. 6 Oh, no! We cooked a Chinese meal last Saturday night. 7 Oh, no! We visited her about four weeks ago. 8 Oh, no! We watched television the day before yesterday.

67
1 No, he didn't. He interviewed him on Tuesday morning at 10.15. 2 He attended the opening of Trinity Hospital on Monday afternoon at 2.00. 3 He visited the BBC Television Centre on Monday morning at 9.00. 4 No, he didn't. He discussed new projects with Mr Short on Wednesday morning at 9.30.
5 He attended the press conference at Heathrow Airport on Tuesday afternoon at 2.15. 6 Yes, he did. He phoned him on Friday afternoon at 4.00.

68
1 Where did Steve attend a press conference on Tuesday? 2 When did Steve phone Scotland Yard? 3 What did he discuss with Mr Short on Wednesday? 4 How many times did he phone Lord Harley's secretary before the interview? 5 At what time did he visit the BBC Television Centre on Monday? 6 Why did he interview Lord Harley on Tuesday morning?

69
1 Did she go shopping last Friday?
2 Did he stay in the office till 8 pm last night? 3 Did she enjoy Madame Tussaud's museum? 4 Did she finish work at 4 o'clock every day last week? 5 Did they send postcards from Bordeaux? 6 Did he ask a lot of questions at the museum?

70
1 That was on Friday, 25th July.
2 That was on Monday, 21st July.
3 That was on Thursday, 24th July.
4 That was on Tuesday, 22nd July.
5 That was on Wednesday, 23rd July.

71
1 Ali, 13th January 2 Halim, 29th September 3 Chu Wen, 3rd October 4 Annegret, 31st July 5 Juan, 11th November 6 Enrico, 12th April 7 Luisa, 2nd February 8 Mikis, 23rd December 9 Yasuko, 25th August 10 Monika, 4th May 11 Maurice, 22nd June 12 Astrid, 1st February

72
1 The First World War started in 1914. 2 Beethoven composed the 'Eroica' in 1803. 3 Napoleon died in 1821. 4 Henry VIII ruled England from 1509 to 1547. 5 Hitler attacked Russia in 1941. 6 Leonardo painted 'The Last Supper' between 1495 and 1498. 7 The Second World War ended in 1945. 8 The Normans invaded Britain in 1066.
9 Two men walked on the Moon in 1969. 10 Columbus discovered America in 1492.

73
1 On Wednesday I'm going to Birmingham. 2 On Thursday at 9 I'm visiting the Ministry of Transport. 3 On Thursday at 2 I'm interviewing Robert Brewster from the National Union of Teachers.
4 On Friday at 10 I'm attending a new art exhibition at the Thorpe Galleries. 5 On Friday at 12.30 I'm meeting Dr Parker for lunch at the Grand Hotel. 6 On Friday at 4.30 I'm seeing the dentist.

74
1 On Tuesday, Steve is having lunch with Dr Walker. He always eats with him on Tuesdays. 2 Steve usually goes to see the dentist once a year. He is going to see him on Friday. 3 On Saturday, Jill and Steve are playing cards with Mike and Joan. They often invite them on Saturdays. 4 Jill and Steve usually help Steve's father in the garden on Sundays. They are helping him next Sunday again.
5 On 4th August, Steve is driving to Leeds. He goes there twice a month.
6 On 5th August, Steve is meeting Dr Green. He meets him twice a year.
7 Harry travels to Glasgow once a month. He is going there tomorrow.
8 Jill and Steve sometimes wash the car at the weekend. They are washing

it next weekend. 9 The students do an English test once a week. This week, they are doing the test on Friday. 10 Jill is meeting Pam for lunch tomorrow. She has lunch with her on Thursdays.

75
1 Mr and Mrs B come from Essex. They are doing some shopping. 2 Mr C comes from Scotland. He is attending a course. 3 Mr D and his son come from Hull. They are going to a football match. 4 Miss E and her boyfriend come from Brighton. They are going on a weekend trip. 5 Mr F comes from Leeds. He is going for an interview. 6 Mr and Mrs G come from Cambridge. They are flying to Las Palmas from Heathrow Airport. 7 Mr H comes from York. He is doing business for his company. 8 Miss J comes from Sheffield. She is going to a jazz concert. 9 Mr and Mrs K come from Wales. They are visiting friends. 10 Mr L comes from Oxford. He is attending a business meeting.

76
1 don't eat 2 Don't spend 3 Don't talk 4 Don't drop 5 Don't pay 6 don't wash 7 Don't be 8 don't smoke 9 don't open 10 Don't lose

77
1 Yes, she spoke French to the waiters. 2 Yes, he drank wine every day. 3 Yes, the children made new friends. 4 Yes, Pam lay in the sun. 5 Yes, he slept until 10 every morning. 6 Yes, she swam in the sea. 7 Yes, the children learnt some French words. 8 Yes, she bought some souvenirs. 9 Yes, he spent all his money. 10 Yes, they went on excursions.

78
1 Did Pam eat a lot? 2 Did the children write postcards? 3 Did Jeff learn any French? 4 Did Jeff swim in the sea? 5 Did Pam spend a lot of money? 6 Did Pam and Jeff make new friends? 7 Did Jeff buy a lot of souvenirs? 8 Did Pam sleep until 10 every morning? 9 Did Jeff speak French to the waiters? 10 Did Pam drink wine every day?

79
1 Pam didn't drink beer on holiday. 2 We didn't write letters from Bordeaux. 3 Pam didn't swim in the swimming-pool. 4 We didn't go on excursions by taxi. 5 Pam didn't buy expensive presents. 6 We didn't fly first class. 7 We didn't leave Bordeaux in the evening. 8 I didn't spend a lot of money on presents. 9 We didn't meet any English people. 10 I didn't ring you at 8.30.

80
1 No, I didn't, but I made an appointment for Saturday morning. 2 No, I didn't, but I took all the letters. 3 No, I didn't, but I spoke to his secretary. 4 No, she didn't, but she rang me at home. 5 No, I didn't, but I went to the post office. 6 No, he didn't, but he ate all the ham. 7 No, I didn't, but I bought some yogurt. 8 No, I didn't, but I spent a lot of money at the new dress-shop. 9 No, he didn't, but he wrote down the names of two other hotels. 10 No, she didn't, but she thought it was relaxing.

81
1 He was visiting the BBC Television Centre. 2 He was discussing new projects. 3 He was interviewing Sam Jones. 4 He was attending a press conference at Heathrow Airport. 5 He was interviewing Lord Harley. 6 He was attending the opening of Trinity Hospital.

82
1 Steve was cleaning shoes when Jeff rang. 2 Jill was drying her hair when the telephone rang. 3 Steve was walking to the phone when it stopped. 4 The sun was shining

when Pam and Jeff left France. 5 It was raining when they landed at Heathrow Airport.

83
1 Was Jill cooking supper when Steve got home? 2 Was Steve washing up when Jeff arrived? 3 Was Jill rushing to the bus stop when the bus passed her? 4 Was the neighbour's wife playing the piano when Jeff called? 5 Was Steve drinking coffee with Harry when Mr Short called him? 6 Were Jill and Steve watching television when the telephone rang? 7 Was Steve reading the newspapers when Pam called? 8 Was Steve listening to jazz records when the dog next door barked? 9 Was Jill doing her shopping when you saw her? 10 Was it raining when the students went to Madame Tussaud's?

84
Hurry, or we *won't get* there at the right time. Yes, we will. We*'ll take* the car. But it *won't be* quicker. Yes, it will. It*'ll take* about half an hour. OK. I*'ll get* the car.

85
1 I expect he'll wait for us. 2 I'm afraid it'll rain. 3 I suppose it'll be far to walk. 4 I'm sure he'll be quite young. 5 I hope it'll be in a quiet street. 6 I expect it'll be far to walk to work. 7 I think it'll be low. 8 I suppose it'll have gas heating. 9 I'm sure we'll walk up. 10 I expect we'll need new ones.

86
1 If it doesn't suit us, we won't have any problems. 2 If it costs too much, we won't take it. 3 If the estate agent has other suitable flats, we'll see them. 4 If we aren't sure, we'll think about it. 5 If the rent is too high, we'll look at other flats. 6 If it suits us perfectly, we'll take it immediately. 7 If the neighbours have a noisy dog, we'll really feel at home there. 8 If the woman next door plays the piano every day, I'll buy a trumpet. 9 If the neighbours are all quiet people, it'll be ideal. 10 If we don't find a suitable flat, we'll rent a house. 11 If we don't like the colours, we'll decorate it. 12 If it has a self-cleaning oven, Jill will be very pleased. 13 If it is carpeted, we won't need new carpets. 14 If it doesn't have central heating, we won't like it. 15 If the building has a lift, it'll be very convenient.

87
1 Yes, it was bigger than our living-room. 2 No, it wasn't as cosy as our study. 3 Yes, it was darker than our bedroom. 4 No, it wasn't as convenient as our garage. 5 Yes, it is more attractive than our area. 6 Yes, it was smaller than our bathroom. 7 No, it wasn't as noisy as our street. 8 Yes, they were bigger than our windows. 9 Yes, it was smaller than our lift. 10 Yes, it is better than our area.

88
If we take the flat, you'll be much *nearer* to your school. The bus journey to the office won't be much longer *than* twenty minutes. The area is certainly *more convenient* for the buses and the Underground. Yes, the bus connections are *better* than from here. I like it, but the view isn't *as* pleasant *as* from our living-room window. But it's quiet, and that's *more important* than a good view! Noisy neighbours are *worse* than a poor view.

89
1 Steve's salary is higher than Jill's salary. Jill's salary isn't as high as Steve's salary. 2 Steve's office is farther away than Jill's school. Jill's school isn't as far away as Steve's office. 3 The Notting Hill Gate flat is bigger than the Baxters' flat. The Baxters' flat isn't as big as the Notting Hill Gate flat. 4 Jeff is fatter

than Steve. Steve isn't as fat as Jeff. 5 Pam and Jeff have more holidays a year than Jill and Steve. Jill and Steve don't have as many holidays a year as Pam and Jeff. 6 The rent for Steve's flat is more reasonable than the rent for Jeff's flat. The rent for Jeff's flat isn't as reasonable as the rent for Steve's flat.

90

1 The ring cost £90. 2 Jill broke her arm on 2rd January, 1979. 3 She fell down. 4 She caught flu in March. 5 She drove to Scotland with her sister. 6 A man stole their car. 7 Jill's parents gave her a watch for her birthday. 8 She lost it two days later. 9 Jill met Steve at a college party. 10 She said 1979 was a very bad year for her.

91

A thief *stole* bracelets and rings worth £1,000 from Mrs R. Abingdon, of 25 Kay Street, Glasgow. He then *went* to a very expensive restaurant, *ate* a lot, *drank* champagne, and *paid* £50 for the meal. He *drove* to Edinburgh, *left* his car at the airport and *took* the plane to London. He *slept* at his girlfriend's house that night and the next morning *bought* a plane ticket and *flew* to Paris. There he *spent* all the money in a few days. The police first *saw* him near Paris, but *caught* him in the south of France.

92

Yesterday we *had* a good time. We went to Enrico's and we *had* dinner there. What *did you have*? *Did you have* a drink first? *Did you have* coffee later? No, I *didn't*, but María and Juan *did*.

93

Where are the *nicest* restaurants in London? The *most expensive* restaurants are in the West End, and the *cheapest* places are the snack-bars, of course. And the *quickest* places to eat are the self-service restaurants. You'll find some of the *most reasonable* and some of the *cosiest* places there, and some of the *tastiest* food. But where can I find the *most typical* English food?

94

1 the oldest 2 the most intelligent 3 the nicest 4 the best 5 the most enthusiastic 6 the most careful

95

1 A is John's house. 2 B is Charles's house. 3 C is Thomas's house. 4 D is Matthew's house. 5 bigger, smaller 6 the cheapest, the smallest 7 older, newer 8 the most expensive

96

1 They're theirs. 2 Yes, it's his. 3 Yes, they're ours. 4 Yes, it's hers. 5 Yes, they're ours. 6 It's his. 7 Yes, they're hers. 8 They're theirs. 9 Yes, it's mine. 10 Yes, it's hers. 11 Yes, they're his. 12 Yes, it's hers.

97

1 of yours 2 of mine 3 of hers 4 of theirs 5 of yours 6 of theirs 7 of his 8 of hers

98

1 Yes, he has. 2 Yes, they have. 3 Yes, she has. 4 No, they haven't. 5 No, he hasn't. 6 No, she hasn't. 7 Yes, they have. 8 No, he hasn't. 9 Yes, she has. 10 No, they haven't. 11 Yes, he has. 12 Yes, she has. 13 Yes, he has. 14 No, they haven't. 15 No, she hasn't.

99

1 No, he's never been there. 2 No, I've never been there. 3 No, they've never been there. 4 No, she's never been there. 5 No, I've never been there. 6 No, we've never been there. 7 No, he's never been there. 8 No, they've never been there. 9 No, she's never been there. 10 No, we've never been there.

100
1 Has Steve ever been to Glasgow? Yes, he's been there twice. 2 Has Barbara ever been to Paris? No, she's never been there. 3 Have Pam and Jeff ever been to Rome? Yes, they've been there once. 4 Has Jill ever been to Dublin? Yes, she's been there three times. 5 Have Pam and Jeff ever been to Edinburgh? Yes, they've been there three times. 6 Have Jill and Steve ever been to Geneva? Yes, they've been there once. 7 Has Harry ever been to Barcelona? Yes, he's been there twice. 8 Has Jill ever been to Madrid? No, she's never been there. 9 Has Barbara ever been to Madrid? Yes, she's been there three times. 10 Have Pam and Jeff ever been to Barcelona? No, they've never been there.

101
1 I've already cleaned them. 2 I've already polished them. 3 I've already ironed it. 4 I've already washed them. 5 I've already phoned him. 6 I've already dusted them. 7 I've already visited her. 8 I've already emptied it. 9 I've already cooked it. 10 I've already shaved.

102
1 María hasn't looked round all the department stores yet. 2 Annegret and Luisa haven't visited the British Museum yet. 3 Yasuko hasn't walked round Regent's Park yet. 4 Ali and Halim haven't used the Underground yet. 5 Enrico hasn't posted his letters home yet. 6 Maurice hasn't played cricket in England yet. 7 Ali hasn't asked the way yet. 8 Monika and Pascale haven't answered their letters yet. 9 Chu Wen hasn't watched television in England yet. 10 Juan and María haven't listened to the radio yet.

103
1 Halim has just posted a letter. 2 Luisa and Yasuko have just ordered two coffees. 3 Pascale has just cooked her lunch. 4 Ali and Mikis have just missed a bus. 5 Monika has just washed the dishes. 6 Chu Wen has just answered a letter. 7 Maurice and Juan have just arrived. 8 Annegret has just phoned her landlady. 9 Enrico has just received a card from his mother. 10 Jill has just corrected the students' homework.

104
1 listened 2 played 3 walked 4 smoked 5 visited 6 asked 7 arrived 8 received 9 watched 10 typed

Answers: Yes, I have/No, I haven't.

105
Jill *has* just *baked* a cake. She *has* already *washed* and *dried* her hair but she *hasn't changed* her dress yet. Steve *has* just *painted* the kitchen door; he *has* already *repaired* a broken shelf, but he *hasn't cleared* the papers off the table yet. Look, Halim and Ali *have arrived*. They *have* already *parked* their car and they *have* just *crossed* the street.

106
1 flown 2 read (seen and bought are also possible) 3 seen (read is also possible) 4 spent 5 eaten, drunk 6 bought 7 gone 8 taken 9 done, learnt 10 spoken

107
1 come 2 written 3 taken 4 made 5 broken 6 left 7 heard 8 met 9 eaten 10 given

108
I *have* never *been* to Cambridge. Oh, I *went* there last summer. I *did* a language course there. *Have* you ever *been* to Oxford? No, but a friend of mine *stayed* there for a month two years ago. He *enjoyed* it very much.

109
I *haven't seen* her in town, Jeff. She *has been* very busy. The children

have been ill. Last week she *started* an office job, only for the summer months. She *has* never *worked* in an office before, so it's difficult for her. She *has* only *been* there a week, but she *has* already *learnt* a lot about office life.

110
I *went* to a new Indian restaurant last night with Mary. *Have* you ever *been* there? No, but Barbara *has* already *been* there twice. She *loved* it. She says she *has* never *eaten* such delicious Indian food. What *did* you *order*? I *had* a prawn curry and Mary *tried* a Tandoori chicken. They *were* both fantastic.

111
I *have* just *seen* Mr Short. He's angry because you *haven't finished* the report on the bank robbery yet. But I *explained* the reason this morning. The bank manager *hasn't given* me all the details yet. I *have* never *done* a report on a bank robbery before. I *haven't written* many. Last year, I only *wrote* two. *Were* there only two bank robberies last year? No, there *were* more, of course, but Harry usually writes those reports.

112
I *have written* some letters. I *have washed* the car, too. And I also *repaired* the broken shelf yesterday. *Have* you *finished* with the typewriter now? And I *made* the beds after breakfast. *Have* you *painted* the kitchen door? By the way, I *took* your suit to the cleaner's last week. Oh, Harry *has given* me two theatre tickets for tonight. I *have bought* a new dress, so I'll wear it for the theatre.

113
Where has she *gone*? I think she's *gone* to the bank. Where have you *been*? I've *been* to the bank. They've *gone* to Brighton today. We have just *been* to the Tate Gallery. Enrico has just *gone* there, too. Have you already *been* there? Has he *been* here? Enrico has already *gone* to the Tate.

114
I *have to* read technical texts in English and I *have to* write reports. *Do* you *have to* speak English in your job? No, I *don't have to* speak a lot of English. I often *have to* speak English to passengers. We *don't have to* write English, but we *have to* understand and speak it correctly. *Do* you *have to* write letters? No, I *don't have to* write letters, but I *have to* dictate letters to my secretary in English. She *has to* write English shorthand. *Does* she *have to* speak English on the telephone? No, she *doesn't have to* do that.

115
1 María, do you have to write English shorthand? 2 Does Ali have to write reports in English? 3 Do Luisa and María have to read English? 4 Does Monika have to speak to passengers in English? 5 Astrid and Maurice, do you have to write essays in English? 6 Does Enrico have to read English newspapers? 7 Does Luisa have to speak to colleagues in English? 8 Do Halim and Chu Wen have to write scientific reports in English? 9 Maurice, do you have to speak to your teachers in English? 10 Does María's boss have to dictate letters in English?

116
1 No, she doesn't. 2 Yes, I do. 3 No, he doesn't. 4 Yes, they do. 5 Yes, he does. 6 Yes, I do. 7 Yes, he does. 8 No, they don't. 9 No, I don't. 10 No, we don't.

117
I *can* read English texts without difficulty but I *can't* speak fluently. I sometimes *have to* write technical reports in English. *Do* you *have to*

speak English? No, I *don't*, but I want to learn. We *have to* write essays on English literature, but we *don't have to* speak English. I *have to* work hard because I want to learn and I *can't* speak English fluently yet.

118
1 Halim thinks logically, too.
2 Pascale works sensibly, too.
3 Mikis learns methodically, too.
4 María reads enthusiastically, too.
5 Monika pronounces very well, too. 6 Luisa works hard, too. 7 Chu Wen and Monika learn fast, too.
8 Ali writes well, too. 9 Monika always arrives punctually, too.
10 Jill speaks optimistically about her students' ability.

119
1 Yes, she teaches well. 2 Yes, she drives carefully. 3 Yes, he works hard. 4 Yes, he drives fast. 5 No, he doesn't drive nervously. 6 Yes, he writes well. 7 No, he doesn't drink heavily. 8 No, he doesn't work lazily. 9 Yes, she speaks English fluently. 10 No, he doesn't read slowly. 11 Yes, she interprets well. 12 Yes, they all learn fast.

120
1 On Tuesday, he's going to play table tennis with Harry. 2 On Wednesday, he's going to take the car to the garage for a service. 3 On Thursday, he's going to see a flat in Camden Town. 4 On Friday, he's going to send a birthday card to Uncle Jim. 5 On Saturday, he's going to watch a football match on television. 6 On Sunday, he's going to listen to a jazz concert on the radio.

121
1 but he isn't going to clean it. 2 but she isn't going to polish them. 3 but he isn't going to cook them. 4 but he isn't going to dry them. 5 but they aren't going to accept it. 6 but Steve isn't going to read them. 7 but they aren't going to take it. 8 but she isn't going to wear it for school. 9 but they aren't going to buy it. 10 but he isn't going to eat them now.

122
She's going to take a skirt, a pair of jeans, a trouser suit, a white blouse, a pair of white shorts, a red sweater, a pair of yellow pyjamas, a green dress, and a pair of Bermuda shorts.

123
1 Who's going to the library? 2 Who went to the British Museum?
3 Who's coming? 4 Who's going to lunch? 5 Who's gone to Cambridge? 6 Who's waiting?
7 Who ate fish and chips yesterday?
8 Who was here? 9 Who visited the Tower yesterday? 10 Who's been to York?

124
1 something 2 anywhere
3 somewhere 4 anybody
5 Somebody 6 somewhere
7 anybody 8 anything 9 anybody
10 something

125
1 Did *anybody* phone this morning? *Somebody* phoned at 10 o'clock. 2 Is there *anything* on television tonight? Yes, there is *something* about Japan.
3 Was there *anybody* in the bank? No, there wasn't *anybody* there.
4 Are they *anywhere* in the kitchen, Jill? I can't see them *anywhere*. Perhaps they are *somewhere* in the bedroom. If I find them *anywhere*, I'll tell you. 5 They didn't know *anybody* there, and *somebody* spilt wine on Pam's dress.

126
1 Everybody 2 nothing
3 everywhere, nowhere
4 everything 5 Nobody
6 everything 7 everybody
8 nobody, Everybody 9 Nothing
10 everywhere

127

Can you think of *anything* for a present? *Something* not too expensive, of course. I saw a lot of art books in a bookshop *somewhere* near Covent Garden. *Somebody* in the shop will help you. If I see *anything*, I'll tell you. If *anybody* knows, she does. Perhaps she can think of *something*.

128

Nobody is coming this weekend, so let's go out. Let's do *something* on Saturday. We haven't been *anywhere* for a long time. Let's go *somewhere*. I'm sure we haven't seen *everything* in London. But we've been almost *everywhere* in London. *Everybody* at work has been there.

129

1 is 2 are 3 is 4 is 5 is 6 is 7 are 8 is

130

1 How much vinegar is there? Only a little. 2 How much cocoa is there? Only a little. 3 How many sausages are there? Only a few. 4 How much soup is there? Only a little. 5 How many onions are there? Only a few. 6 How much ham is there? Only a little. 7 How many lemons are there? Only a few. 8 How much cheese is there? Only a little. 9 How much salt is there? Only a little. 10 How many potatoes are there? Only a few. 11 How much honey is there? Only a little. 12 How much flour is there? Only a little. 13 How many eggs are there? Only a few. 14 How much milk is there? Only a little. 15 How much ice-cream is there? Only a little. 16 How many biscuits are there? Only a few. 17 How much orange juice is there? Only a little. 18 How many apples are there? Only a few. 19 How much beer is there? Only a little. 20 How many bananas are there? Only a few.

131

1 No, we don't need any rice. 2 Yes, we need some flour. 3 Yes, we need a cabbage. 4 No, we don't need any toothpaste. 5 Yes, we need some soap. 6 No, we don't need a cucumber. 7 No, we don't need any bread. 8 Yes, we need some writing paper. 9 No, we don't need a note-pad. 10 Yes, we need some milk.

132

We don't need *any* orange juice. We haven't got *many* potatoes. I don't need *any* milk. We haven't got *any* biscuits. We haven't got *much* beer. I don't have to buy *any* tomatoes, but we haven't got *many* apples. And we haven't got *much* butter. We haven't got *any* chocolate and we haven't got *any* cream.

133

She bought three cans of beer, half a pound of butter, a tube of toothpaste, two tins of soup, a carton of cream, half a pound of bacon, a jar of coffee, two bars of chocolate, a loaf of bread, and a bottle of tomato ketchup.

134

1 Yes, he's got an American one. 2 He's got some leather ones. 3 Yes, he's got a Japanese one. 4 He's got some cashmere ones. 5 Yes, he's got an English one. 6 Yes, he's got a portable one. 7 He's got a black one. 8 He's got some silk ones. 9 He's got some linen ones. 10 Yes, he's got an automatic one.

135

1 The white ones. 2 The one with the zip fastener. 3 The big ones. 4 The leather ones. 5 The blue one. 6 The cotton ones. 7 The white ones. 8 The check ones. 9 The cheaper one. 10 The one in the red cover.

136
1 that 2 who 3 that 4 who 5 who, that 6 who 7 that 8 who 9 that 10 who, that

137
1 Is that the chair that broke? 2 Is that the man who owns the garage round the corner? 3 Is that the girl who lives in the flat above Harry's? 4 Is that the man who has been to Australia? 5 Is that the picture that cost over £3000? 6 Is that the lady who went to Pam's party? 7 Is that the man who repaired our washing-machine? 8 Is that the woman who opened a dress shop in Duke Street? 9 Is that the wine that is very strong? 10 Is that the lamp that was very expensive?

138
Suggestions: 1 The Bay is a hotel near Aberdeen that is 300 years old/that has 150 beds/that serves a five course dinner for £9.50. 2 The Crown is a hotel near Plymouth that is only 2 years old/that has 100 beds/that offers first class accommodation for £21 a night/that serves a three course lunch for £6.50. Mr Croft is the man who owns the Crown Hotel. 3 The Embassy is a luxury hotel near Brighton that has a golf course and a heated swimming-pool/that has a dinner dance on Saturday evenings/that offers bed and continental breakfast from £28. Mr Lang is the man who manages the Embassy Hotel. 4 Mill House is a guest house in the Lake District that has 25 beds/that offers good walking and fishing/that costs £7.50 for bed and breakfast/that offers full board for £72 a week. Mrs Robbins is the woman who owns the Mill House guest house. 5 The White Hart is a motel near Cardiff that is only one year old/ that has 60 beds/that costs £12 a night. Mrs Hall is the woman who manages the White Hart Motel.

Note: *which* instead of *that* is possible throughout.

139
I hate parties, but that was one of the worst ( ) Mary has ever had. There were a lot of people there *who* drank too much, and there were a lot of people ( ) I didn't know. I liked the couple *who* own the restaurant, but I didn't like the man *who* was an architect. He talked about his work all the time, and that's one thing *that* really annoys me! The most exciting person ( ) I saw there was *you.*

140
1 The ashtray I'm going to give to my mother cost almost £8. 2 That glass vase you bought at Harrod's is very attractive. 3 Those red sandals we saw at Saxone's were very comfortable. 4 That black handbag I liked best was too expensive. 5 These pyjamas I bought at Selfridge's are good quality. 6 These books we bought at Foyle's were cheap. 7 The blue shirt you bought in Oxford Street was reasonable. 8 The shopping-bag I bought for my mother is very useful.

141
1 who 2 who 3 who 4 whose 5 ( ) 6 whose, whose 7 who 8 who, ( )

Solution: Charles killed John.

142
1 who's (who has) 2 whose 3 whose 4 Who's, (who is), who's (who is) 5 who's (who is) 6 whose 7 whose 8 whose 9 Who's, (who is), who's (who is) 10 whose

143
1 We haven't played tennis for five years. 2 We haven't visited your parents since May. 3 We haven't played cards with Penny and Graham for weeks. 4 We haven't seen an opera since 'Tosca'. 5 We haven't watched television since last Friday. 6 We haven't phoned Helen and Jim

for about five weeks. 7 We haven't visited an art gallery for over a year. 8 We haven't invited Harry and Mary to dinner since March. 9 We haven't walked round Hyde Park for years. 10 We haven't cooked a pizza since Sally and Bob were here.

144
1 I haven't washed them for five weeks. 2 I haven't cleaned them since Tuesday. 3 I haven't made one since your birthday. 4 I haven't cooked one since last week. 5 I haven't painted it for three years. 6 I haven't washed it for over a week. 7 I haven't watered them for three days. 8 I haven't bought one for two years. 9 I haven't ironed since last Friday. 10 I haven't washed them since your parents stayed with us.

145
1 Jill would like to go to Scotland. 2 Steve would like to go to the cinema. 3 I'd like to go skiing. 4 We'd like to go to Paris. 5 Jill and Steve would like to go to a concert. 6 They'd like to go on holiday. 7 Jill would like to go swimming. 8 I'd like to go for a drive in the country. 9 Steve would like to go to an Indian restaurant. 10 We'd like to go for a walk in Hyde Park.

146
1 Would you like a cup of tea? 2 Would you like to watch television? 3 Would you like a glass of beer? 4 Would you like to look at this magazine? 5 Would you like to visit an art gallery? 6 Would you like a piece of cake? 7 Would you like to spend a weekend in Edinburgh? 8 Would you like a new coat? 9 Would you like to listen to the radio? 10 Would you like to have lunch in town?

147
1 She hasn't been to Scotland for two years. 2 He hasn't been to the cinema since he saw 'Dr Zhivago'. 3 I haven't been skiing since the holiday in Austria. 4 We haven't been to Paris for five years. 5 Jill and Steve haven't been to a concert since last autumn. 6 They haven't been on holiday since last summer. 7 Jill hasn't been swimming since she went with Pam six weeks ago. 8 I haven't been for a drive in the country since Mary stayed with us. 9 Steve hasn't been to an Indian restaurant for four weeks. 10 We haven't been for a walk in Hyde Park since your mother visited us.

148
1 You've had the car since last Wednesday / for five days, Mr and Mrs Patten. That's £175, please. 2 You've had the car since last Thursday / for four days, Mrs Willis. That's £70, please. 3 You've had the car since yesterday / for one day, Mr and Mrs Parker. That's £139, please. 4 You've had the car since last Tuesday / for six days, Miss Lane. That's £115, please. 5 You've had the car since last Saturday / for two days, Mr Henderson. That's £80, please. 6 You've had the car since last Monday / for seven days, Mr and Mrs Green. That's £165, please. 7 You've had the car since last Tuesday / for four days, Mr Butcher. That's £80, please. 8 You've had the car since yesterday / for one day, Miss Donovan. That's £12, please. 9 You've had the car since last Friday / for three days, Mr and Mrs Lord. That's £80, please. 10 You've had the car since last Saturday / for two days, Miss Carpenter. That's £30, please.

149
1 He prefers to go by train. 2 He has promised to clean the car. 3 We intend to go to Stratford on Avon next weekend. 4 We are planning to go to Scotland for a holiday. 5 I hope to hear from Jeff. 6 She wants to learn German. 7 He has offered to help us. 8 He likes to go for a drink

at "The Globe". 9 Jill has promised to wait for Steve. 10 We expect to have a letter from our parents.

150
1 Can I use your phone, please? 2 Can I borrow your sewing-machine, please? 3 Can we leave early, please? 4 Can we stay up late, please? 5 Can I have another piece of cake, please? 6 Can we invite some friends to tea, please? 7 Can I use your pen, please? 8 Can I copy your notes, please? 9 Can we go to the library, please? 10 Can I borrow your car, please?

Note: *may* (more formal) instead of *can* is possible throughout.

151
1 Yes, you can. 2 Yes, you can. 3 No, I'm afraid you can't. 4 No, I'm afraid you can't. 5 No, I'm afraid you can't. 6 Yes, you can. 7 Yes, you can. 8 Yes, you can. 9 No, I'm afraid you can't. 10 No, I'm afraid you can't.

152
1 Can I have two eggs, Jill? Yes, you can have two eggs once a week. 2 Can I have a grapefruit, Jill? Yes, you can have a grapefruit every day. 3 Can I have a glass of beer, Jill? No, I'm afraid you can't. 4 Can I have a cup of coffee and a cake, Jill? No, I'm afraid you can't. You can have a cup of black coffee, but you can't have a cake. 5 Can I have an apple, Jill? Yes, you can have an apple every day. 6 Can I have a cup of tea with sugar, Jill? No, I'm afraid you can't. You can have a cup of tea, but you can't have sugar. 7 Can I have a slice of bread and jam, Jill? No, I'm afraid you can't. You can have a slice of bread once a week, but you can't have jam. 8 Can I have meat, vegetables and salad, Jill? Yes, you can have 150 grams of meat, vegetables or salad every day. 9 Can I have a bar of chocolate, Jill? No, I'm afraid you can't. 10 Can I have fish, potatoes, and a glass of wine? No, I'm afraid you can't. You can have 150 grams of fish every day, you can have two potatoes once a week, but you can't have wine.

153
1 Jill bought Steve's mother a cardigan. 2 I asked the policeman the time. 3 I've sold Jeff my old camera. 4 Jill has made Steve a chocolate cake. 5 Barbara gave Steve her address. 6 Pam passed Jeff a newspaper. 7 Jeff has lent Steve some money. 8 Steve will send Uncle Bill a birthday card. 9 Jill tells Steve the truth. 10 Jill cooked Steve a pizza.

154
Suggestions: Shall we go to Cambridge? Shall we stay at a guest house? Shall we go by train? Shall we visit Bath? Shall we book a big hotel with bath? Shall we stay at a small hotel without bath? Shall we go by bus? etc.

155
1 Shall I help you? 2 Shall I lend you my car? 3 Shall I repair your car? 4 Shall I drive you home? 5 Shall I give you a five-pound note?

156
1 Swimming is fun. 2 Reading is relaxing. 3 Smoking is unhealthy. 4 Cooking is interesting. 5 Driving fast is dangerous. 6 Shopping is boring. 7 Riding is fun. 8 Diving is difficult. 9 Skiing is enjoyable. 10 Dancing is fun.

157
1 Can you ride, Monika? Yes, I enjoy riding. 2 Can you cook, Pascale? Yes, I enjoy cooking. Can you knit, Pascale? No, I hate knitting. 3 Can you skate, Annegret? No, I hate skating. 4 Can you swim, Yasuko? Yes, I enjoy swimming. Can you sew, Yasuko? No, I hate sewing. 5 Can

you dive, Astrid? Yes, I enjoy diving. Can you paint, Astrid? No, I hate painting. **6** Can you drive, Halim? Yes, I enjoy driving. Can you dance, Halim? No, I hate dancing.

158

1 Pam wants Jeff to do the shopping. **2** She wants Kate to dust the furniture. **3** She wants Mark to clean the shoes. **4** She wants the children to take the dog for a walk. **5** She wants Jeff to buy some flowers. **6** She wants Kate to water the plants. **7** She wants Jeff to make the beds. **8** She wants Mark to feed the fish. **9** She wants the children to dry the dishes. **10** She wants Jeff to hoover the carpets.

159

1 Pam would like you to do the shopping. **2** She would like me to dust the furniture. **3** She would like him to clean the shoes. **4** She would like us to take the dog for a walk. **5** She would like you to buy some flowers. **6** She would like her to water the plants. **7** She would like me to make the beds. **8** She would like you to feed the fish. **9** She would like us to dry the dishes. **10** She would like me to hoover the carpets.

160

Solution: María, Juan, Enrico, Luisa, Maurice

1 They all want María to make the food. **2** Enrico wants Luisa to invite the guests. **3** María wants Juan to do the shopping. **4** Juan wants Enrico to get the records. **5** Luisa wants Enrico and Maurice to buy the beer.

Index